Homemade Ice Cream Recipes

100 Yummy Desserts For Your Ice Cream Maker

MATT PYNE

ISBN-13:978-1973969303

ISBN-10:1973969300

DEDICATION

To Roselyn, Love you much!

TABLE OF CONTENTS

INTRODUCTION

What's better than running your fingers around the sides of an ice cream freezing bowl and tasting the fresh and flavorful ice cream you've just made in the comfort of your home? Hmmm... still thinking? Truly, making ice cream at home is fun! Eating it is even more exciting! That's because ice cream is a dessert that's so tasteful and refreshing with a range of flavors that you can never get tired of.

As a matter of fact, ice cream is the ultimate treat, enjoyed everywhere and served in many different ways. Whether it's to enjoy at a birthday, dinner or beach party or served in a cup, a cone or double cone, ice cream goes with everything and it's the perfect treat for any season. Ice cream is a delight. It drives away sadness and lightens up the faces of everyone who takes it.

Radiate happiness in your home by making it a first-class ice cream shop. Even if you aren't an ice cream expert, you will soon become one by following the recipes presented in this book. Simply pick up any good inexpensive and user-friendly ice cream maker for home use and freeze away.

Other frozen desserts of interest are:

Gelato: is a silky Italian ice cream. It is really creamy because it's made with whole milk and cream and contains less than 55% air. It can be made in an array of flavors. From everyone favorite chocolate and strawberry, to fresh and exciting flavors like hazelnuts, pistachio, cake batter or dulce deleche. The exciting thing about it is that during the summer you can use any seasonal fruit to make the most wonderful fruit ice cream and other frozen dessert. Fruits like blueberry, mango, watermelon and cantaloupe can also be used. Gelato is really refreshing.

Sorbet: Formerly used as a refresher between courses, sorbet has grown in popularity and is currently enjoyed as a dinner desserts in many homes. The reasons are due to its simplicity, availability of ingredients and lower fat content as compared to the traditional desserts. It is simple to make, uses a few regular ingredients and contains limited fat.

Various seasonal fruits can be used but note that the taste of sorbets depends to a large extent, on the ripeness and sweetness of the fruit or juice used. You could use sugar in place of tart fruit or take out the sugar entirely if the fruit is very ripe. Once frozen, the ice cream will not taste as sweet as the mixture did.

The Electric Ice Cream Maker

There are different types of electric ice cream makers in the market that are convenient, affordable and easy to use. They all come with a freezer bowl and a paddle that is run with an electric motor. The basic components of an electric ice maker/ machines are:

Base: This is where the motor is housed. It is also where the electrical cord is stored.

Controls: Most models only have a simple on-off dial that is located on the front of the base. A few others have additional features like timers and options for changing the speed of the motor.

Freezer Bowl: Most ice cream makers come with a removable bowl that is insulated with a specially formulated cooling liquid. Once the liquid is completely frozen and the bowl is rotating inside the machine, the wet mixture content is turned to ice cream or sorbet.

The bowl must be kept frozen ahead of time. Therefore, it is advisable to keep the bowl in the freezer when it isn't being used. This way, you are always set to make a batch of ice cream at any time.

Dasher (also called paddle or mixing arm): This is a plastic blade that sits inside the freezer bowl. Its function is to rotate the wet mixture (ice cream custard), stirring and scraping it until the mixture becomes frozen

Lid: this covers the ice cream maker when in use. It fits firmly on top of the freezer bowl, snapping into place with ease and helping to prevent splashes and contain the cold. The lid can either be opaque or transparent. However, It is better to go for transparent kind for easy monitoring.

Spout: That hole on the lid that enables you add to your frozen desserts; nuts, fresh fruits, cookies and any other extra ingredients during the last minutes of mixing.

Note that most components of the ice cream machine aren't dishwasher - safe. It is advisable to hand wash in warm soapy water only.

Other Equipment For Making Ice Cream:

Ice cream and frozen dessert making requires little equipment; most of whom are everyday utensils. Here are a few helpful but not mandatory ones:

Rubber spatula: perhaps this is the most important tool. It is used for scraping ice cream from the canister and to smoothen icing and topping over the finished ice cream.

Digital scale: for measuring ingredients.

Blender or Food Processor : to puree fruit for ice cream and sorbet.

Candy Thermometer: for monitoring the sugar changes when it is being heated.

Small instant-read thermometers: ensure it measures up to 260F.

Mixer (handheld or countertop): for mixing egg yolks and sugar together. It also helps to blend other common ingredients that are used.

Using an Electric Ice Cream Maker in Your Kitchen

Using an ice cream maker is easy. Simply follow these basic steps:

First, get the freezer bowl frozen by wrapping in a plastic bag and freezing until completely frozen. This should take at least 15 hours. The bag is necessary as it helps to keep the bowl from freezer burn. Once frozen, place the bowl into the ice cream maker and add the dasher or paddle to the freezer bowl. Turn your machine on and pour in your chilled ice cream ingredients. Replace lid and then wait for 20-30 minutes to enjoy your frozen dessert.

Scoop out immediately from the freezer bowl with a rubber spatula so it doesn't freeze to the sides. If you like your ice cream soft, enjoy immediately. But, if you desire firm consistency, remove the ice cream to a freezer- safe bowl and freeze another 3-4 hours. Do not forget to store your ice cream and sorbets in air-tight containers that are also freezer-safe so as to prevent freezer burn. On no account should you store them in the freezer bowl.

Benefits of Using an Electric Ice Cream Maker:

Making your own ice cream and sorbets comes with several benefits. This includes:

1. It saves you money on buying treats from the store.

2. You can say good bye to additives and preservatives that are contained in many store-bought desserts.

3. There are so very many flavors and flavor combination for you to try.

4. You can enjoy recipes that are easy to adapt in order to make sugarless treats for specialty diets.

5. With an electric maker machine, there is no need to add salt and ice when making ice-creams as opposed to the old-style manual machines.

6. It saves on counter and freezer space.

7. It makes us happy and removes the stress of the day. Ice-cream fuels the production of thrombotonin (the happiness hormone) in the body.

8. It is also healthy. Did you know that? It is a huge source of vitamins and minerals like calcium sand phosphorus. It is loaded with carbs, protein and fat which provide energy. However, eat in moderation and choose flavors wisely!

Making Ice Cream

Ice creams must have smooth creamy texture, and for this to be achieved, the water molecules and fat globules in the mixture have to be evenly suspended to prevent ice crystals from forming (or keep them small) during freezing. Using basic ice cream ingredients enables this to happen, and this is one advantage of making ice creams at home. We use fresh wholesome ingredients unlike manufacturers of commercial ice cream who use emulsifiers and stabilizers to cover up or make up for inferior ingredients used, increase the shelf life of their products as well as to improve the texture.

These basic ingredients (cream, eggs, milk and sugar) also add flavor. Nevertheless, you can substitute any of them with ingredients that are similar. It all depends on your preferences. For instance, you could use any cream but there may be differences in texture and flavor. Have it in mind however, that the butterfat in the cream is responsible for its rich smooth texture. The more butterfat there is, the smoother and richer the ice cream. The richer the cream; the richer the finished product.

Heavy cream is the richest as it contains about 36% fat. Whipping cream contains 30% fat, light cream or coffee; 18% while half-and-half contain 10% fat. The general ratio is 50 percent cream to 25 percent milk. (It is advisable to always use half-and-half as base for the cream because it is pasteurized and homogenized as well. Heavy cream is pasteurized only).

Pre-Chilling

Your ice cream mixture can never be too cold. For best results, ice cream mixture must be pre-chilled and mix thoroughly before churning. Chill in the refrigerator or over an ice-water bath for speedier result. If the mixture is warmer than 100F when the freezing process starts, it will cause an increase in the churning time and this will lead to a production of butter flecks which can damage the fine texture of your homemade ice cream. In the event that butter forms in a batch of ice cream, put the ice cream in the refrigerator to melt. Once melted, remove the butter by passing it through a strainer and then refreeze.

Expansion During Freezing

Do not fill the ice cream maker to the full. Only fill three –quarters of the way full. This is because as the ice cream freezes, it will expand little. You do not want your ice cream to spill over the sides. Additionally, the ice cream needs air to aerate as it is churned (overrun) because this improves the finished ice cream texture and prevents it from solidifying as ice block.

Storing And Serving Temperatures

To prolong shelf life, store ice cream and other frozen desserts at low temperatures, between 0-10 F. this will improve their texture as well. Before serving, warm ice cream a little; a temperature of about 30F is ideal for serving.

If the ice cream container is frozen firmly, refrigerate for about 30 minutes before serving or let it stay at room temperature for about 10 minutes. Watch, so the ice cream does not over thaw as repeated thawing and freezing will weaken its texture.

Ripening And Eating

You can make ice cream custard bases ahead of time, up to 2 full days before the ice cream is to be frozen and left in the freezer for several hours before serving. This 'ripening' process improves its texture and enables the flavors to blend well.

Homemade ice cream should only be kept frozen for a couple of days and no more. Otherwise, ice cream crystals may develop on top and assumes a heavy, unpleasant texture. Nevertheless, this may never happen. Homemade ice creams are so delicious; you won't need to keep for too long!

Since homemade ice creams do not contain ingredients used making commercial ones, they tend to get frozen very quickly. Consequently, if making ice cream to serve much later, remove from out freezer about 15 - 20 minutes before serving so that it can be scooped easily.

Adding Extracts, Mix-ins & Alcohol

For the best flavor, add extracts such as vanilla, almond and maple after the ice cream mixture has cooled, but before churning. Mix-ins such as candy pieces, nuts and chocolate chips should be added at the last minutes of churning when the ice cream is already done or starting to solidify but not up to desired consistency. This ensures an even distribution.

If using alcohol, add to the ice cream machine only minutes before total freezing, as alcohol can interfere with freezing process. Additionally, add alcohol in moderation. Do not add more than ¼ a cup in a recipe that yields a quart. In addition, the finished ice cream must be chilled further to achieve a firm consistency.

Now let's give everyone something to scream about with these yummy flavors below. Put your best ice cream maker to work by trying them out now!

Vanilla Flavored Ice Cream

Preparation time: 30 minutes (plus 2 hours chilling time)

Cooking time: 20 minutes

Servings: 8

Ingredients:

3 cups half and half

1/3 cup of sugar

3 egg yolks

1 tbsp of vanilla extract (or 2 vanilla bean pods with the seeds scraped)

Directions:

1. Mix vanilla extracts or bean with the half and half; simmer for about 15 minutes in big pot over medium heat. Strain the mixture then set aside.

2. Beat the egg yolks, sugar and salt together in a big bowl until it becomes smooth.

3. Fold in 1 cup of the half and half mixture into the egg batter until even. Now, whisk this batter into the remaining half and half mixture in the pot.

4. Heat over medium-low heat and cook, stirring consistently along the base of the pot to make sure everything is cooking. Take out the pot from heat immediately it reaches 170°F, then strain through a fine-mesh strainer into a bowl.

5. Place the bowl of ice cream in an ice bath then chill to room temperature. Pop the base into the fridge and chill for 2 hours.

6. Churn in an ice cream maker, immediately the base is chilled. Scoop the ice cream into a container when the texture is between soft serve and freeze ice cream. Freeze until it becomes hard.

Vanilla Lemon-Olive Oil Ice Cream

Preparation time: 30 minutes (plus 2 hours chilling time)

Cooking time: 20 minutes

Servings: 8

Ingredients:

3 cups half and half

1/3 cup of sugar

3 egg yolks

1 tbsp of vanilla extract (or 2 vanilla bean pods with the seeds scraped)

¼ cup of olive oil

1 teaspoon lemon zest

Directions:

1. Mix vanilla extracts or bean with the half and half; simmer for about 15 minutes in big pot over medium heat. Strain the mixture then set aside.

2. Beat the egg yolks, olive oil, sugar, lemon zest and salt together in a big bowl until it becomes smooth.

3. Fold in 1 cup of the half and half mixture into the egg batter until even. Now, whisk this batter into the remaining half and half mixture in the pot.

4. Heat over medium-low heat and cook, stirring consistently along the base of the pot to make sure everything is cooking. Take out the pot from heat immediately it reaches 170°F, then strain through a fine-mesh strainer into a bowl.

5. Place the bowl of ice cream in an ice bath then chill to room temperature. Pop the base into the fridge and chill for 2 hours.

6. Churn in an ice cream maker, immediately the base is chilled. Scoop the ice cream into a container when the texture is between soft serve and freezer ice cream. Freeze until it becomes hard.

Caramel Ice Cream

Preparation time: 30 minutes (plus 2 hours chilling time)

Cooking time: 20 minutes

Servings: 8

Ingredients:

3 cups half and half

1/3 cup of sugar

3 egg yolks

1 tbsp of vanilla extract (or 2 vanilla bean pods with the seeds scraped)

½ cup salted caramel

Directions:

1. Mix vanilla extracts or bean with the half and half; simmer for about 15 minutes in big pot over medium heat. Strain the mixture, add the salted caramel then set aside. Reduce the sugar, if desired, to make it less sugary.

2. Beat the egg yolks, sugar and salt together in a big bowl until it becomes smooth.

3. Fold in 1 cup of the half and half mixture into the egg batter until even. Now, whisk this batter into the remaining half and half mixture in the pot.

4. Heat over medium-low heat and cook, stirring consistently along the base of the pot to make sure everything is cooking. Take out the pot from heat immediately it reaches 170°F, then strain through a fine-mesh strainer into a bowl.

5. Place the bowl of ice cream in an ice bath then chill to room temperature. Pop the base into the fridge and chill for 2 hours.

6. Churn in an ice cream maker, immediately the base is chilled. Scoop the ice cream into a container when the texture is between soft serve and freezer ice cream. Freeze until it becomes hard.

Rose Pistachio Classic Ice Cream

Preparation time: 30 minutes (plus 2 hours chilling time)

Cooking time: 20 minutes

Servings: 8

Ingredients:

3 cup of half and half

1/3 cup sugar

3 egg yolks

1 tbsp of vanilla extract (or 2 vanilla bean pods with the seeds scraped)

¼ cup pistachio cream

½ cup coarsely diced pistachios

1 teaspoon rose water

Directions:

1. Mix vanilla extracts or bean with the half and half; simmer for about 15 minutes in big pot over medium heat. Strain the mixture. Pour in the rosewater and diced pistachios then set aside.

2. Beat the egg yolks, pistachio cream, sugar and salt together in a big bowl until it becomes smooth.

3. Fold in 1 cup of the half and half mixture into the egg batter until even. Now, whisk this batter into the remaining half and half mixture in the pot.

4. Heat over medium-low heat and cook, stirring consistently along the base of the pot to make sure everything is cooking. Take out the pot from heat immediately it reaches 170°F, then strain through a fine-mesh strainer into a bowl.

5. Place the bowl of ice cream in an ice bath then chill to room temperature. Pop the base into the fridge and chill for 2 hours.

6. Churn in an ice cream maker, immediately the base is chilled. Scoop the ice cream into a container when the texture is between soft serve and freezer ice cream. Freeze until it becomes hard.

Cake Mix Ice Cream

Preparation time: 45 minutes (plus 2 hours freezing time)

Cooking time: 10 minutes

Servings: 8

Ingredients:

3 cups of half and half

1 cup milk

¼ teaspoon salt

1 cup sugar

¾ cup yellow cake mix

6 tablespoons rainbow sprinkles (optional)

Directions:

1. Heat milk and sugar mixture in a small pot over medium heat for some time; stir from time to time until the sugar is almost completely dissolved.

2. Mix milk-sugar batter with cake mix, half and half, and salt in a mixing bowl. Stir the mixture properly to combine. Refrigerate for about 30 minutes.

4. Once chilled, transfer to your ice cream maker and churn according to manufactures directions.

16

5. Add the sprinkles then let it mix for another 5 minutes.

6. Scoop out ice cream from the ice cream maker into a small container or a glass bowl. Use a foil or lid to cover then freeze for another 2 hours to overnight until the ice cream is firm.

Caramel-Pecan Classic Ice Cream

Preparation time: 15 minutes (plus 1 hour 50 minutes freezing time)

Cooking time: 5 minutes

Servings: 8

Ingredients:

14 oz. sweetened condensed milk

5 oz. evaporated milk

2 tbsp sugar

2 tsp vanilla

2 cups whole milk

¼ cup caramel sauce

½ cup semisweet chocolate morsels

1 tsp shortening

¾ toasted diced pecans

Directions:

1. Beat the milks, sugar and vanilla together in a large bowl until smooth. Cover and refrigerate for 30 minutes.

2. Pour the chilled milk batter into the freezable container of your electric ice cream maker then freeze, following the manufacturer's directions.

3. Mix the caramel sauce into the already-made ice cream. Take out the freezable container containing the ice cream from the ice-cream maker then freeze for 15 minutes.

4. Nuke the chocolate morsels and shortening in the microwave at high for 1 minute then mix until even.

5. Set the toasted diced pecans on a baking sheet lined with parchment paper. Sprinkle melted chocolate on top and freeze for 5 minutes. Crush into small pieces then fold into the ice cream.

6. Scoop ice cream into an airtight container and freeze for about 1 to 1½ hours until hard.

Buttermilk Ice Classic Cream

Preparation time: 30 minutes (plus 4 hours freezing time)

Cooking time: 10 minutes

Servings: 10

Ingredients:

2 cups buttermilk

2 cups heavy whipped cream

8 large egg yolks

1 cup sugar

1 cup crème fraîche

2 tbsp fresh lemon juice

¼ tsp salt

Directions:

1. In a heavy medium saucepan, bring cream to a simmer. Beat the egg yolks and sugar in a medium bowl until smooth.

2. Fold the hot cream gradually into the egg yolk batter. Pour the mixture into the saucepan and heat over medium-low heat. Stir often for about 3 minutes until thick enough to stay on the back of spoon but do not boil.

3. Strain the mixture through a fine strainer into a clean bowl then cool to room temperature. Fold in the buttermilk, lemon juice, crème fraiche and salt. Refrigerate until chilled.

4. Once chilled, transfer the ice cream to your ice cream maker and process according to the manufacturer's directions. Scoop the ice cream into containers, cover and freeze for at least 4 hours or until hard.

Cooking tip: This ice cream can be made 3 days ahead of time. Freeze and thaw slightly at room temperature before serving.

Vanilla Flavored Funfetti Ice Cream

Preparation time: 30 minutes

Cooking time: 0 minute

Servings: 6

Ingredients:

2 cups heavy whipped cream

1 cup half and half

¾ cup white sugar

2/3 cup funfetti cake mix

1 teaspoon vanilla extract

1 teaspoon rainbow sprinkles

Directions:

1. In your ice cream maker, combine the heavy cream, sugar, half-and-half, cake mix and vanilla.

2. Process according to the manufacturer's directions or until the ice cream texture looks like soft serve.

3. Scoop out the ice cream and garnish with rainbow sprinkles and desired sauces. Serve.

Green Tea Classic Ice Cream

Preparation time: 10 minutes (plus 6 hours chilling time)

Cooking time: 15 minutes + chilling time

Servings: 2 to 4

Ingredients:

2 cups of half and half

3 tablespoons green tea powder

½ cup sugar

Pinch of Salt

Directions:

1. First, freeze the ice cream bowl for 24 hours.

2. In saucepan, mix the sugar and half and half together then cook on medium heat.

3. Pour in the green tea powder and continue mixing until it foams but do not boil.

4. Pour ice into a large bowl.

5. Pour the ice cream batter into a smaller bowl then place it on the bowl filled with ice.

6. Cool the ice cream; cover with a plastic wrap then refrigerate for 3 hours.

7. Transfer the ice cream to your ice cream maker and churn according to the manufacturer's directions.

8. Once the ice cream is ready, scoop into an air tight container and freeze for 3 hours.

Serve.

Creamy Maple Syrup Ice Cream

Preparation time: 30 minutes (plus 3 hours freezing time and overnight chilling)

Cooking time: 15 minutes

Servings: 4 cups

Ingredients:

¾ cup maple syrup

6 egg yolks

1½ cups of half and half

1 cup cream

1 tsp Kosher salt

Directions:

1. Beat the egg yolks and maple syrup together in a heavy-bottomed medium saucepan. Fold in the cream and half and half, and cook over medium heat.

2. Cook for 10 to 15 minutes and whisk often until the mixture is thick enough to coat the back of the spoon. Stir in the salt then strain into an airtight container. Refrigerate for at least 6 hours or overnight.

3. The following day, churn the ice cream in your ice cream maker according to the manufacturer's directions. Scoop the churned ice cream into an airtight container then freeze for at least 3 hours. Serve.

NUT FLAVORED ICE CREAM

Nutty Pistachio Ice Cream

Preparation time: 45 minutes (plus 8 hours freezing)

Cooking time: 15 minutes

Servings: 6

Ingredients:

¾ cup pistachios, roughly diced

1 1/3 cups of shelled pistachio nuts

¾ cup sugar

2 cups heavy cream

1 cup of whole milk

Pinch of salt

6 large egg yolks

½ tsp almond extract

1 tsp vanilla extract

Directions:

1. Blend the pistachios nuts in the food processor until finely processed but not into a paste. Set aside.

2. Warm up the milk, 1 cup of cream, sugar and salt in a medium saucepan; stir until the sugar dissolves. Fold in the finely ground nuts, cover, then remove from the heat. Let it steep for at least 30 minutes.

3. Strain the nut mixture, pressing the nuts to bring out liquid then throw away the solids.

4. Pour the cream-milk mixture into the saucepan. Pour the remaining cream into a large bowl then place a mesh strainer over it.

5. Get another medium bowl, beat the egg yolks together. Pour the warmed milk-cream mixture slowly into the whisked egg yolks. Beat consistently then scrape the egg yolks into the saucepan.

6. Use a heatproof spatula to stir everything together over medium heat, scrape the base as you stir until the mixture thickens and coats the spatula.

7. Strain the custard using the strainer then stir it into the cream. Add the almond and vanilla extract then stir until well mixed.

8. Refrigerate until chilled. Transfer to your ice cream maker and freeze according to the manufacturer's instructions.

9. Once churned, whisk in the diced pistachios with a rubber spatula.

Cooking tips: The ice cream will not be brightly green because it's natural without food coloring. You may add few drops of green food coloring to get a deep green shade.

Black Walnut Flavored Ice Cream
Prepare tasty walnut ice cream any day.

Preparation time: 15 minutes (plus 4 hours freezing)

Cooking time: 15 minutes

Servings: 4 cups

Ingredients:

2/3 cup black walnuts, coarsely diced

4 - 5 egg yolks

2 cups of cream

2/3 cup sugar

2 cups milk

½ vanilla bean, scraped

Directions:

1. In a heavy deep pot, heat the cream, milk, walnut pieces and sugar to 170°F until it steams but not simmer. Turn off the heat then add the vanilla bean, scraped insides then stir properly, cover and cool for an hour.

2. Transfer the walnut-cream blend to a container and chill for at least 4 hours or overnight.

3. Remove vanilla bean and walnut pieces from the mixture by straining. Keep the Walnut pieces and refrigerate.

4. Heat up the sieved mixture to 160°F.

5. Meanwhile, whisk the egg yolks to combine. When the cream is heated and reaches its temperature, temper the eggs so they don't scramble.

6. Use one hand to hold the ladle and the other to whisk the egg yolks. Add a little hot cream with one hand and continue beating intensely with the other hand. Add 2 ladles full and then pour the cream-egg combination into the pot and stir properly. Cook slowly, stirring frequently for 5 minutes but don't simmer.

7. Strain the mixture again and refrigerate at least to room temperature then pour into your ice cream maker. Churn until you get the texture of soft-serve. Transfer to a large bowl and fold in the kept walnut pieces gently. Freeze and serve!

Honey Macadamia Nut Ice Cream

Preparation time: overnight (plus 5 hours freezing time)

Cooking time: 5 minutes

Servings: 4

Ingredients:

2¼ oz. honey roasted macadamia nuts

2 tablespoons unsalted butter

½ teaspoon salt

1 teaspoon vanilla extract

2/3 cup sugar

1½ cups of milk

1½ cups of heavy cream

Directions:

1. Put the freeze bowl for the ice cream maker in the freezer a day before making the ice cream. Chop the macadamia nuts roughly or finely if preferred.

2. Melt the butter in a small saucepan then add the diced nuts; sauté for a minute over medium-low heat.

3. Add milk, vanilla extract and salt then stir until well combined. Add the sugar then heat for a minute. Don't overheat the milk but just heat to dissolve the sugar. Do not simmer or boil. Turn off the heat and let it cool.

4. Transfer the mixture into a 2 quart pitcher then add the heavy cream then stir to mix well.

5. Chill completely in the refrigerator overnight; this will help make the ice cream texture finer and also blend the flavors in.

6. On the next day, set the frozen freezer bowl in your ice cream maker then turn on the machine. Pour the nut mixture into the bowl and churn for 15 to 20 minutes, until you get a soft serve texture.

7. Scoop the ice cream into a plastic container then freeze for 4 to 5 hours until hard enough to scoop.

8. Scoop, and enjoy!

Cooking tips: Store any leftover in a container then wrap with a terrycloth dishtowel and freeze. This will keep the ice cream texture soft and easy to scoop.

Maple Flavored Nutty Ice Cream

Make that dinner unforgettable by treating your family to this maple flavored nut ice cream as dessert.

Preparation time: 30 minutes (plus chilling time)

Cooking time: 12 minutes

Servings: 6

Ingredients:

¾ cup chopped nuts

¾ cup brown sugar

2 cups milk

2 eggs, slightly beaten

2 cups whipping cream

2 - 3 teaspoons maple flavor

Directions:

1. Mix eggs, milk and brown sugar together in a medium saucepan then mix properly. Cook for about 12 minutes over medium heat or until slightly thickened and coats the back of the metal spoon, stirring consistently. Do not boil the mixture. Cool for 30 minutes.

2. Add the whipping cream and maple flavor then blend well. Stir in the nuts and refrigerate until you are ready to freeze.

3. Transfer ice cream to your ice cream maker and freeze according to the manufacturer´s instructions.

Grape-Nut Flavored Ice Cream

Preparation time: 15 minutes (plus 6 hours freezing time)

Cooking time: 15 minutes

Servings: 4 cups

Ingredients:

1 cup grape nuts cereal

2 cups heavy cream

6 egg yolks

1 cup whole milk

2/3 cup sugar

1 vanilla bean (about 4 inch)

¼ tsp salt

Directions:

1. Whisk the egg yolks lightly in a medium bowl then set aside.

2. Mix cream, sugar and milk together in a medium-size saucepan. Divide the vanilla bean lengthwise then scrape out the seeds with the tip of a knife.

Pour the seeds into the cream mixture; add a pinch of salt and whisk irregularly. Heat over medium low heat until it starts to bubbles around the edges of the pan.

3. Remove the mixture from heat then pour into the whisked eggs, adding one tbsp at a time, continue whisking until the eggs are tempered.

4. When the cream and egg yolk mixture have been well blended, pour into the saucepan and heat over medium-low heat until the custard is thick enough to coat the back of the spatula or spoon. The custard should read 170°F to 175°F and make sure you don't overheat.

5. Pour the custard into a medium-size bowl then place on an ice bath. Cool at room temperature for 1 hour, stirring once in a while. Cover then refrigerate for another 2 hours or overnight until completely cold.

6. Once chilled, transfer the ice cream to your ice cream maker and churn according to the manufacturers' directions. During the last 5 minutes of churning time, add the grape nuts.

7. Scoop out the ice cream into a container or bowl big enough to contain 1 quart. Cover and freeze for at least 3 hours until firm. Serve

Nutty Buttered Pecan Ice Cream

Enjoy the goodness of pecan in this delicious nutty buttered pecan ice cream.

Preparation time: 30 minutes (plus 2 hours chilling time)

Cooking time: 30 minutes

Servings: 18 (½ cup each)

Ingredients:

For the ice cream:

2 cups whole milk

4 egg yolks

1½ cups brown sugar

Pinch of salt

2 tablespoons unsalted butter

2 cups of half and half

2 cups whipping cream

2 teaspoon vanilla extract

For the candied butter pecans:

1 cup pecans

⅓ cup of sugar

2 tablespoons unsalted butter

Directions:

1. To make the ice cream; whisk the egg yolks, milk, brown sugar and salt together in a medium-size saucepan then heat over medium-high heat until

it simmers. Reduce the heat to medium then whisk for 5 minutes or until it starts to thicken.

2. Strain through a fine mesh strainer into a large bowl then beat in butter until well mixed. Add the half and half, vanilla and cream; mix until it incorporates. Cover with a plastic wrap and chill in the refrigerator for about 2 hours.

3. To make the candied butter pecans; Mix the pecans, butter and sugar together in a heavy skillet and heat over medium heat, stirring often for about 6 minutes or until the sugar dissolves completely and is browned.

6. Remove the mixture from heat then spread out the nuts on a foil to cool. Once cooled, crush into small pieces and set aside.

7. Transfer the ice cream mix to your ice-cream maker and process according to manufacturer directions. Once ready, stir in the pecans kept aside and serve.

Gluten-Free Cashew Flavored Ice Cream

It's simple to make with only 3 ingredients. It's the best ice cream every birthday party should have. Yummy!

Preparation time: 25 minutes (plus2 hours freezing time)

Cooking time: 0 minute

Servings: 6

Ingredients:

2 cups roasted no-salt-added cashews, soaked overnight

2 cups vanilla almond milk, unsweetened

½ cup pure maple syrup

Directions:

1. Soak the cashews in water overnight.

2. The next day, drain then pour into a high powered blender.

3. Add 1 cup of almond milk and puree on low to medium speed for some minutes. Increase the processing speed gradually to high speed until the mixture is frothy smooth.

4. Pour in the remaining milk and syrup then blend until well mixed.

5. Pour the mixture into your ice cream maker then churn until it becomes soft serve.

6. Scoop the ice cream into a container then freeze for about 1 to 2 hours to become hard.

7. Let the ice cream thaw a bit on the counter for 5 to10 minutes before you serve.

Creamy Chestnut Ice Cream

Preparation time: 30 minutes

Cooking time: 20 minutes

Servings: 8

Ingredients:

¼ cup milk

5 oz. sweetened chestnut puree

½ cup superfine sugar

6 egg yolks

2 tbsp rum (optional)

1/3 cup heavy cream

4 oz. marrons in syrup (optional)

Directions:

1. In a pan, combine chestnut puree, milk and 3 oz. of the sugar then bring to a boil over medium heat.

2. In a bowl, beat the egg yolks and the remaining sugar together until it become light.

3. Pour the boiling milk into the egg yolks and whisk consistently; pour the combination back into the pan.

4. Stir with a wooden spoon over low heat until it coats the back of the spoon lightly. It should leave a clear path when you draw a line with your finger on the coated spoon.

5. Now, remove the pan from the heat then pour into a bowl. Pour in the rum if using.

6. Place the bowl of ice cream on the ice bath and stir occasionally to hinder skin formation.

7. Once chilled, strain the custard through a chinois or fine strainer into your ice cream maker then churn for 10 to 15 minutes.

8. Pour the mixture in a slow stream into your ice cream maker and churn for another 10 minutes or until firm and creamy.

9. Top ice cream with marrons in small pieces, if desired, or sprinkle with semi-sweet or plain chocolate sauce.

Brazil Nut Vanilla Ice Cream

Preparation time: 20 minutes (plus 2 hours chilling time)

Cooking time: 0 minute

Servings: 4

Ingredients:

2 cups unsweetened Brazil nut milk

2/3 cup soaked raw cashews (or ½ cup raw cashews, soaked for 8 - 12 hours, drained and rinsed)

½ cup agave nectar or honey

2 vanilla beans, seeds only

2 tsp vanilla extract

1/8 tsp salt

Directions:

1. Pour ½ cup of Brazil nut milk and all the cashews into a blender and puree until finely smooth. Pour in the remaining Brazil nut milk, all the honey, vanilla bean seeds, vanilla extract and salt then blend until well processed.

2. Pour the mixture into a jar then refrigerate for at least 2 hours to 48 hours. Once chilled, pour the mixture in your ice-cream maker and freeze according to the manufacturer's instructions.

3. This ice cream tastes best when consumed immediately but you may store leftovers for up to 5 days in an airtight container and freeze. Thaw slightly for some minutes before serving.

Coconut Flavored Ice Cream

Preparation time: 30 minutes (plus 6 hours freezing and chilling time)

Cooking time: 0 minute

Servings: 4 (1 quart)

Ingredients:

27 oz. coconut milk, chilled

½ - 1 cup amber maple syrup, Grade A to taste (or ⅓ - ½ cup of honey + coconut milk at room temperature for easy blending)

Pinch of sea salt

1 tbsp vanilla extract

Directions:

1. Whisk coconut milk and preferred sweetener together with a blender or by hand until well blended.

2. Chill the mixture for 2 hours (if the coconut milk isn't chilled) before using the ice cream maker.

3. Once chilled, pour the mixture into your ice cream machine then freeze for 20 to 30 minutes or according to manufacturer directions. Stop freezing when the mixture becomes frosty and thick. It should sit on the spoon and not slip off.

4. The ice cream is ready when its texture is soft serve. Scoop ice cream into a container then freeze for another 4 hours or until firm.

5. When ready to eat, use a wooden spoon to remove the ice cream from the container.

Cooking tips: Use maple syrup in place of honey for a vegan version.

If you are using honey, blend the coconut milk at room temperature with the liquid honey. Melt the honey first on low heat, if using solid honey. Refrigerate the mixture before freezing it in your ice cream maker.

FRUIT FLAVORED ICE CREAM

Creamy Lemonsicle

Preparation time: 20 minutes (plus 2 hours freezing time)

Cooking time: 0 minute

Servings: 12 (½ cup each)

Ingredients:

6 tablespoons fresh lemon juice

2½ cups whole milk

2 teaspoons lemon zest

1¾ cups sugar

1 cup whipping cream

Directions:

1. Combine all the ingredients in a large bowl then whisk everything together until the sugar dissolves.

2. Pour cream into your ice-cream maker then process according to manufacturers' directions.

3. Place in the freezer for at least 2 hours and then serve.

Orange Fruity Ice Cream

Preparation time: 30 minutes (plus freezing time)

Cooking time: 0 minute

Servings: 3 cups

Ingredients:

2 cups freshly squeezed orange juice, strained to remove pulp

1½ cups heavy whipping cream

1 tbsp orange zest (optional)

½ cup half and half

½ cup granulated white sugar, or to taste

1 tsp pure vanilla extract

1 tbsp fresh lemon juice

Directions:

1. Mix all the ingredients in a measuring cup or a large bowl. Cover then refrigerate for some hours or overnight until completely chilled.

2. Pour the cream into the container of your ice cream maker then process according to the manufacturer's directions.

3. Once ready, scoop the ice cream into a cold container and freeze.

4. Refrigerate the ice cream for 30 minutes to soften, if it too firm. Serve.

Cooking tip: half and half cream is a combination whole milk and cream and it has 10% to 12% butterfat. Heavy cream/heavy whipping cream has about 36% to 40% butterfat.

Apple Flavored Ice Cream

Ditch the ice cream shop and prepare a delicious apple flavored ice cream at home!

Preparation time: 20 minutes (plus 1 hour 30 minutes chilling time)

Cooking time: 5 minutes

Servings: 12

Ingredients:

3 medium apples, peeled, cored and sliced

2 cups heavy whipping cream

½ cup sugar

1 cup milk

¼ tsp salt

3 egg yolks, whisked

1 tsp vanilla

½ cup sugar

1 tbsp lemon juice

Red/ green food coloring (optional)

Directions:

1. In a 1 quart saucepan, combine egg yolks, milk, ½ cup of sugar and salt then cook over medium heat, stirring consistently until about to boil but do not boil.

2. Pour mixture in a cold bowl then refrigerate uncovered for 1 to 1½ hours or until room temperature.

3. Fold in the whipping cream, 3 to 4 drops of food coloring and vanilla.

4. Pour half of the apples, lemon juice and ½ cup of sugar into the blender. Cover then process until roughly chopped using the quick on-and-off method. Pour in the remaining apples, cover then process until properly chopped but not mashed.

5. Stir the apple puree into the milk batter. Pour the cream into 2 quart ice cream maker and freeze according to manufacturer's instructions.

Snickerdoodle Apple Pie Ice Cream

Preparation time: 12 hours

Cooking time: 30 minutes

Servings: 4 cups

Ingredients:

For the Apples:

2 medium Granny Smith apples, peeled, cored and sliced into 1" sizes

1 tbsp no-salt-added butter

¼ cup light brown sugar

1 tsp ground cinnamon

For the ice cream:

1¾ cups of heavy cream

5 egg yolks

¾ cup whole milk

1/3 cup granulated sugar

¼ tsp kosher salt

½ cup diced snickerdoodle cookies

1 tsp vanilla extract

Directions:

1. To prepare the apples: in a medium-size skillet, heat up butter and brown sugar over medium heat. Once the butter melts and becomes bubbly, add the sliced apples and cinnamon then cook, stirring often for 10 to 15 minutes or until the apples become soft and about all the liquid has vanished. Remove from heat then cool. Refrigerate in a sealable container until when you are ready to use.

2. To make the ice cream; whisk the egg yolks in a medium-size bowl, then whisk in 2½ tbsp of sugar then set aside.

3. Combine the cream, milk, the remaining sugar and the salt in a medium saucepan then stir and heat over medium-high heat. Once the batter starts to simmer, lower the heat to medium.

4. Spread some of the hot cream batter into the egg yolk mixture and whisk consistently. Do this again then stir the cream in the saucepan with a rubber spatula, while slowly pouring the cream-egg yolk mixture in the bowl into the pan.

5. Cook the batter over medium heat, stirring consistently until thickened, reads 170 to 175°F on a thermometer and coats the back of a spatula. Pass the ice cream base through a fine-mesh strainer into a clean bowl then place on an ice water bath. Stir once in a while until cooled; cover and refrigerate overnight.

6. To churn the ice cream; once the ice cream is ready to be pureed, pour the cooked apples, vanilla and half of the ice cream base into a food processor then process until smooth.

7. Pour the processed ice cream and the remaining ice cream into the bowl of your ice cream maker then freeze according to the manufacturer's directions. During the last minute of churning time, add the diced cookies or you can as well fold in the cookies with your hand after churning.

8. Scoop the ice cream into a freezer-safe container then store in the freezer.

Apple Cinnamon Flavored Ice Cream

Preparation time: 20 minutes (plus 4 hours chilling and freezing time)

Cooking time: 5 minutes

Servings: 6 to 8

Ingredients:

For the ice cream base:

1 teaspoon ground cinnamon

2 ¼ cups heavy cream

1 cup milk

¾ cup powdered sugar

½ teaspoon sea salt

1 tablespoon pure vanilla extract

For the apple cinnamon swirl:

2 large apples, peeled, cored, and cut into small chunks

2 tablespoons no-salt-added butter

¼ teaspoon ground cloves

1 teaspoon ground cinnamon

¼ teaspoon ground nutmeg

¼ cup brown sugar

Directions:

1. To make the cream base; whisk the milk, cream, sugar, salt and cinnamon together in a mixing bowl until well mixed. Cover and place in the refrigerator for at least 2 hours until completely cold.

2. While chilling the milk mixture, in a skillet, melt the butter over medium heat. Combine the apples with sugar and spices then toss. Add the seasoned apples to the skillet then cook, stirring irregularly for about 2 to 3 minutes until the apples becomes soft. Remove from heat then cool. Cover and refrigerate.

3. Before making the ice cream, beat the cream base for some times then pour into a 1½ quart ice cream maker; churn for about 20 to 25 minutes or until the ice cream is fluffy, frozen and has a soft-serve texture. When it's about 3 to 5 minutes before churning time ends, or when the ice cream is almost ready, add the apple-cinnamon mixture and proceed with churning.

4. Once ready, spoon the ice cream into freezer-safe containers, cover and freeze for 1 to 2 hours until firm.

Blueberry Flavored Ice Cream

Preparation time: 20 minutes (plus freezing and 2 hours chilling time)

Cooking time: 5 minutes

Servings: 4 cups

Ingredients:

2 cups blueberries, picked-over

1½ cups heavy cream

1 cup milk

¾ cup sugar

1/8 tsp salt

Directions:

1. Bring the blueberries, salt and sugar to a boil in a saucepan over moderate heat then crush berries, using a fork to stir. Let it simmer, stirring often for 5 minutes then slightly cool.

2. Pour the mixture into a blender then add the milk and purée until smooth. Stir in the cream and strain through a strainer into a clean bowl, using the back of a spoon to press on the solids. Cover and refrigerate the cream for at least 2 hours to 1 day or until chilled.

3. Once chilled, pour the cream into your ice-cream maker and freeze.

4. Once ready, scoop the ice cream into an airtight container then freeze until firm. This ice cream can be made about a week ahead of time.

Blackberry Flavored Ice Cream

Preparation time: 35 minutes (plus 2 hours chilling time)

Cooking time: 12 minutes

Servings: 8 (½ cup each)

Ingredients:

2 cups fresh blackberries, rinsed

1 cup whipping cream

1 cup half and half

1 cup sugar, divided

1 egg yolk

1/8 tsp cinnamon

½ tsp vanilla

Directions:

1. In a small saucepan, combine the blackberries and ½ cup of sugar then bring to a low boil and simmer for 5 minutes to melt the sugar and crush the berries. Cool slightly then process in your blender. Strain the mixture

through a fine strainer to remove the seeds. Throw away the seeds then set the liquid mixture aside.

2. In a small saucepan, whisk the egg yolk, ½ cup of half and half, and the remaining ½ cup of sugar together then cook over low heat, stirring consistently for about 5 minutes or until the mixture boils and slightly thickens.

3. Whisk in the remaining half and half, all the cream, vanilla and cinnamon into the cooked mixture then whisk in the strained blackberry mixture.

4. Let it cool then refrigerate the cream base for 1 to 2 hours or overnight.

5. Pour the chilled cream base into your electric ice cream maker then churn for 25 minutes.

6. Serve or scoop into an airtight container and freeze.

Lemony-Blackberry Ice Cream

Preparation time: 30 minutes (plus 1 hour freezing time)

Cooking time: 0 minute

Servings: 8 cups

Ingredients:

3 cups half and half

2 cups blackberry puree

¼ cup lemon juice

1 tbsp lemon zest

14 oz. sweetened condensed milk

Directions:

1. Mix all the ingredients in a large bowl. Strain through a fine strainer into a clean bowl, for an extra smooth ice cream. Discard the seeds.

2. Pour the mixture into your ice cream maker and churn according to the manufacturer's directions.

3. Once churned, scoop the ice cream into an airtight container and freeze for at least 1 hour to firm before serving.

Strawberry Flavored Ice Cream

Preparation time: 50 minutes (plus 3 hours chilling time)

Cooking time: 0 minute

Servings: 6 cups

Ingredients:

2 cups heavy cream

1 lb. strawberries, trimmed, cut in halves if large

¾ tsp fresh lemon juice

¾ cup sugar

1/8 tsp salt

Directions:

1. In a large bowl, crush the strawberries with lemon juice, sugar and salt roughly with a potato masher, stirring and crushing for 10 minutes.

2. Pour half of the mashed strawberry mixture into your food processor then add cream and blend until smooth. Pour the pureed mixture back into the bowl with the remaining strawberries and refrigerate, stirring once in a while for 3 to 6 hours until very chilled.

3. Once cold, Pour into your ice cream maker and freeze.

4. When ready, scoop ice cream into an airtight container and freeze to harden.

Pineapple Flavored Ice Cream

Preparation time: 40 minutes (plus 16 hours of cooling and freezing)

Cooking time: 20 minutes

Servings: 6 cups

Ingredients:

1½ cups crushed pineapple in juice, drained (keep ½ cup + 1 tbsp of the juice)

¾ cup + 2 tbsp sugar

2 tsp cornstarch

1¼ cups whole milk

2 large egg yolks

¼ tsp vanilla

1 cup heavy cream, chilled

Directions:

1. In a 2 to 3 quart heavy saucepan, bring pineapple, ½ cup of sugar and ½ cup of the reserved pineapple juice to a boil, stirring until the sugar melt.

2. Lower the heat then simmer; stir occasionally for 5 minutes until the pineapple becomes soft.

3. In a small bowl, stir the cornstarch and the remaining tbsp of pineapple juice together until the cornstarch dissolves. Pour the cornstarch mixture into the pineapple blend and simmer; stir regularly for about a minute until it becomes thick.

4. In a 1½ to 2 quart heavy saucepan, bring milk to just a boil. Whisk the egg yolks, a pinch of salt and the remaining ¼ cup + 2 tbsp of sugar together in a bowl then pour in hot milk in a stream and then whisk.

5. Pour the creamy egg yolk mixture back into the saucepan then cook over medium-low heat, stir with a wooden spoon for 2 to 3 minutes, until the cream reads 170°F to 175°F on the thermometer.

6. Strain the cream immediately through a fine-mesh strainer into a clean bowl then stir in the pineapple mixture and vanilla. Cool to room temperature, stirring once in a while. Stir in the cream then cover and chill for about 4 hours until completely cold.

7. Once chilled, pour the cream into your ice cream maker then freeze.

8. When ready, scoop the ice cream into an airtight container then freeze for at least 12 hours to firm up.

Cooking tip: This ice cream can be made 3 days ahead.

Coconut-Pineapple Flavored Ice Cream

Enjoy this creamy coconut pineapple flavored ice cream made right at home. So yummy!

Preparation time: 30 minutes (plus 4 hours freezing time)

Cooking time: 0 minute

Servings: 6

Ingredients:

15 oz. coconut cream

1 cup coconut milk, unsweetened

½ cup whole milk

2 tablespoons pineapple juice

1 cup unsweetened or sweetened coconut flakes, + ¼ cup for garnish (optional)

¾ cup finely diced fresh pineapple (or canned mashed pineapple)

Directions:

1. In a large mixing bowl, mix coconut cream, whole milk, coconut milk and pineapple juice together. Pour in the coconut flakes then stir to mix well.

2. Pour the mixture into your ice cream maker then freeze according to the manufacturer's directions.

3. When it's about 5 minutes before freezing time ends, add the pineapple.

4. When ready, scoop the ice cream into an airtight container then freeze for at least 3 to 4 hours or overnight to get best results.

5. Garnish ice cream with toasted coconut flakes, if desired then serve.

6. To make toasted coconut flakes; preheat your oven to 325°F. Spread the coconut flakes on a parchment paper lined baking sheet evenly then bake in the oven for about 15 to 20 minutes. Check and toss the coconut every 5 to 7 minutes so they don't burn. Remove from the oven when evenly golden then set aside to cool.

Banana Flavored Ice Cream

Preparation time: 30 minutes (plus 2 hours freezing time and overnight chilling)

Cooking time: 5 minutes

Servings: 24 (½ cup each)

Ingredients:

4 – 5 medium ripe bananas, mashed (or 2 cups mashed)

4 cups half and half cream

5 oz. evaporated milk

2½ cups sugar

4 cups heavy whipping cream

Dash of salt

4 eggs, whisked lightly

1 tbsp vanilla extract

Directions:

1. Heat the half and half in a large heavy saucepan to 175°F then stir in the sugar and salt until it dissolves. Whisk a little quantity of the hot mixture into the eggs then pour into the pan, whisking consistently. Cook and stir over low heat until mixture gets to 160°F and coats the back of a metal spoon.

2. Remove the mixture from heat then cool immediately by setting the pan in a bowl of ice water then stir for 2 minutes. Stir in the milk, whipping cream and vanilla then cover with a plastic wrap with it touching the surface of the mixture. Refrigerate for some hours or overnight.

3. Once chilled, stir in the bananas and pour into the cylinder of your ice cream maker about 2/3 full. Churn according to the manufacturer's instructions.

4. Refrigerate the remaining cream until you are ready to freeze.

5. After churning, scoop the ice cream into a freezer container then freeze for 2 to 4 hours before serving.

Tasty Cherry Flavored Ice Cream

Preparation time: 30 minutes

Cooking time: 0 minute

Servings: 8

Ingredients:

1 cup dark sweet cherries, frozen

¼ cup cherry juice concentrate

2 tsp almond extract

½ cup fat-free milk

1 cup vanilla low-fat yogurt

1 cup heavy cream

½ cup white sugar

1 pinch of salt

Directions:

1. Pour the milk, heavy cream, yogurt and cherry juice into the bowl of your blender. Add the cherries, sugar, almond extract and salt then process until just little bits of the cherries are left.

2. Pour the mixture into your 1½ quart ice cream maker then churn according to the manufacturer's instructions.

Flavored Grape Ice Cream

This ice cream is so different from all other grape ice creams you've tasted. It is easy to make, delicious and healthy.

Preparation time: 30 minutes

Cooking time: 0 minute

Servings: 10

Ingredients:

12 oz. grape juice concentrate, frozen and thawed

2½ cups sugar

½ cup fresh lemon juice

12 oz. evaporated milk

2 cups half and half, (or light cream)

2 cups milk

Directions:

1. Melt the sugar in the grape juice then add the lemon juice.

2. Mix the mixture with cream, milk and evaporated milk.

3. Pour the cream into your 1 gallon ice cream maker then freeze according to manufacturer's directions.

Yummy Peach Flavored Ice Cream

Preparation time: 40 minutes (2 hours chilling time)

Cooking time: 0 minute

Servings: 4 cups

Ingredients:

2 cups peaches, finely diced

1¼ cups sugar

½ lemon, juiced

2 large eggs

2 cups whipping cream (or 2 cups heavy cream)

1 cup milk

Directions:

1. In a bowl, mix the peaches, lemon juice and ½ cup of sugar together.

2. Cover the bowl then refrigerate for 2 hours, stirring every 30 minutes.

3. Take out the bowl of mixture from the fridge then drain into another clean bowl.

4. Put the drained mixture back to the fridge. In a mixing bowl, whisk the eggs together for 1 to 2 minutes until fluffy and light.

5. Beat in the remaining ¾ cup of sugar, adding a little at a time then whisk continuously for about a minute until well combined.

6. Pour the milk and cream into the mixture then whisk to completely blend.

7. Pour in the chilled peach juice and mix until well blended.

8. Pour the cream into your ice cream maker then churn according to the manufacturer's directions.

9. When it's about 2 minutes before churning time ends or after the ice cream stiffens, add the peaches and continue churning until ready.

CHOCOLATE FLAVORED ICE CREAM

Chocolaty Ice Cream

Preparation time: 43 minutes (plus 8 hours chilling time)

Cooking time: 15 minutes

Servings: 6 cups

Ingredients:

1½ oz. (½ cup) cocoa powder, unsweetened

8 large egg yolks

3 cups half and half

9 oz. sugar

1 cup heavy cream

2 tsp raw vanilla extract

Directions:

1. In a medium saucepan, heat up the cocoa powder and 1 cup of half and half over medium heat then whisk to blend. Pour in the remaining half and half and the heavy cream then bring to just a simmer, stirring often; remove from heat.

2. Whisk the egg yolks in a medium mixing bowl until it becomes light. Add the sugar slowly then whisk to blend well. Add the cream mixture gradually, tempering it until 1/3 of the cream mixture has been added.

3. Pour in the remaining cream mixture into the saucepan then cook over low heat. Continue cooking, stirring often until the mixture becomes a little thick, and gets to 170°F to 175°F and coats the back of a spoon.

4. Transfer the mixture to a container then cool for 30 minutes at room temperature. Add the vanilla extract then stir. Refrigerate the mixture; when its chilled enough not to create condensation on the lid, cover then refrigerate for 4 to 8 hours or until it reaches 40°F or lower.

5. Once chilled, pour the mixture into your ice cream maker then churn for 25 to 35 minutes or according to the manufacturer's instructions.

6. Serve as soft serve or freeze for another 3 to 4 hours to firm up.

Chocolaty Flavored Coconut Ice Cream

Preparation time: 30 minutes (plus 5 hours chilling and freezing time)

Cooking time: 15 minutes

Servings: 6 cups

Ingredients:

½ cup coconut flakes, unsweetened

2/3 cup cocoa powder, unsweetened

3 cups coconut milk, unsweetened

3 tbsp agave syrup

1¼ cups sugar

3 large egg yolks

1 tbsp pure vanilla extract

Directions:

1. Place a fine-mesh strainer in a large bowl then place it over a bowl filled with ice water.

2 Whisk the agave syrup and coconut milk together in a large saucepan and heat over medium-low heat until warm.

3. Whish the cocoa powder and sugar together in a medium heatproof bowl then whisk in a cup of the warmed coconut milk gradually until smooth then whisk in the egg yolks.

4. Scrape the cocoa puree into the saucepan then beat until well combined. Cook the mixture over medium heat, beating consistently for about 6 minutes, until very hot and slightly thick but do not boil. Strain the mixture immediately through a strainer into already prepared bowl then stir in the vanilla. Stir until chilled.

5. Once chilled, transfer the cream to your ice cream maker then freeze according to the manufacturers' instructions.

6. When ready, scoop the ice cream into a big plastic container then freeze for at least 4 hours or until hard.

7. Toast the coconut flakes in a small skillet over low heat for 4 minutes or until a bit browned. Transfer the toasted flakes to a platter then cool. Top ice cream with toasted flakes and serve.

Chocolate Strawberry Ice Cream

Preparation time: 50 minutes (plus 12 hours of chilling and freezing)

Cooking time: 10 minutes

Servings: 10

Ingredients:

8 oz. dark chocolate chips

4 cups strawberries, hulled and chopped

1 cup white sugar, divided

1 tbsp lemon juice

2 cups heavy whipping cream, divided

1 cup whole milk

6 egg yolks

1 tsp vanilla extract

1 pinch of salt

Ice cubes

Directions:

1. Puree the strawberries, lemon juice and ¼ cup of sugar in your blender until roughly chopped. Pour the mixture into a bowl then refrigerate for about an hour or until very cold.

2. In a saucepan, heat up the milk, 1 cup of heavy cream and ¾ cup of sugar over medium-low heat for about 5 minutes or until warmed through. Remove the mixture from heat, cover then cool for 30 minutes.

3. In a bowl, beat the egg yolks together then pour in the cream mixture slowly, whisking consistently. Pour the warmed egg mixture back into the saucepan.

4. Heat up the egg mixture over medium heat, stirring frequently for about 5 minutes, scraping the bottom of the saucepan, until it becomes thick enough to coat the back of a spatula.

5. Pour the remaining cup of heavy cream into a big bowl then place a strainer over it. Now, pass the warm egg custard through the strainer slowly then stir. Add the vanilla extract and salt then stir in chilled strawberry mixture and chocolate chips into the cream.

6. Pour ice cubes into a bowl then add water and stir. Set the bowl containing strawberry and chocolate mixture in the ice bath then cool to room temperature for about 10 minutes, stirring often. Take out the bowl of ice cream from the ice bath then cover with plastic wrap. Refrigerate for 8 hours to overnight or until very cold.

7. Once chilled pour the cream into your ice cream maker then churn according to manufacturer's instructions or until you get a soft-serve texture.

8. When ready, scoop the ice cream into a sealable container, cover with a plastic wrap then seal. Let the ice cream ripen in the freezer for about 2 hours or overnight for best results.

Crunchy Chocolaty Toffee Ice Cream

Preparation time: 4 hours 20 minutes

Cooking time: 4 minutes

Servings: 8

Ingredients:

1 cup sugar

¼ cup cocoa powder, unsweetened.

2 cups whipping cream

1 cup milk

1 tsp vanilla

1/8 tsp salt

¾ cup chocolate-covered English toffee bar

Directions:

1. Mix cocoa powder with sugar in large bowl then add the milk, whipping cream, vanilla, and salt; stir everything together until the sugar melt.

2. Pour the cream-cocoa mixture into the freezer container of your 1 or 1½ quart ice cream maker. Churn according to the manufacturer's instructions. Stir in the toffee pieces and ripen the ice cream for about 4 hours, if desired.

3. To make the chocolate cones: An interesting way of making this is, placing ½ cup of the semisweet chocolate chips in a microwave-safe bowl then nuke, uncovered for a minute at medium-high heat or 70% power then stir.

4. Microwave for another 1½ to 3 minutes or until the chocolate dissolves and is smooth; stir every 15 seconds then scoop the chocolate on top of the ice cream cones, covering about 1/3 of each cone. Stir in 1 tsp of dissolved shortening, if the chocolate is very thick. Set the cones on a waxed paper lined baking sheet with the top sides down. Refrigerate the cones for about 15 minutes or until ready.

Pecan Chocolate Ice Cream

Preparation time: 40 minutes (plus 2 hours chilling time)

Cooking time: 8 minutes

Servings: 8

Ingredients:

8 oz. bittersweet chocolate, diced

7 oz. bittersweet chocolate, diced

2 cups whipping cream

2 cups half and half

6 large eggs yolks

1¼ cups toasted pecans, diced

½ cup sugar

Directions:

1. Stir 8 oz. of chocolate in a double boiler placed over simmering water until it completely melts and becomes smooth. Remove melted chocolate from the water then boil the cream and the half and half in a heavy big saucepan.

2. In a medium-size bowl, beat the yolks and sugar until well blended then whisk in the hot cream mixture gradually then pour the batter back into the saucepan. Heat up the mixture over medium-low heat, stirring for about 3 minutes until it becomes thick enough to coat the back of the spoon but do not boil.

3. Pass the custard through a strainer into a clean large bowl then whisk in the dissolved chocolate; cover and refrigerate for about 2 hours until chilled.

4. Add 7 oz. of the diced chocolate and pecans to the custard then churn in your ice cream maker according to the manufacturer's directions. When ready, scoop the ice cream into a container then freeze.

Note: This ice cream can be made 3 days ahead.

Almond Chocolaty Ice Cream

This homemade ice cream recipe is yummy and tastes heavenly.

Preparation time: 40 minutes (plus 2 hours chilling time)

Cooking time: 15 minutes

Servings: 8

Ingredients:

4 tbsp cocoa powder

1½ cups almonds, toasted

4 cups heavy cream

1½ cup sugar

4 oz. baking chocolate, shaved

2 cups whole milk

½ tsp salt

6 egg yolks

2 tsp vanilla extract

Directions:

1. Heat up the milk, sugar, cocoa powder and salt in a large saucepan over medium heat, continue stirring then bring to a simmer but do not boil.

2. Whisk the egg yolks slightly in another bowl then stir in about ¾ cup of the hot chocolate mixture.

3. Transfer the yolk mixture with the remaining chocolate mixture to the saucepan.

4. Heat up the mixture until it becomes thick but don't boil. Remove from heat then stir in the shaved chocolate.

5. Pour the mixture into a glassy bowl then refrigerate for about 2 hours and stir occasionally.

6. Once chilled, whisk in 4 cups of cream and the vanilla then pour everything into your ice cream maker; churn according to the manufacturer's instructions.

7. To churn the ice cream, place the container in the bucket, with the dasher inside then place the motor on top of the ice cream can lid then plug it in.

8. Add ice and rock salt in layers while the machine is running. Layer about 2" of ice, followed by about ¼ cup of rock salt; repeat this until you have ice on top, churning while adding the ice or else it may not start properly.

9. While churning the ice cream, make the almond toast. Lay out the almonds on a cookie sheet then bake for about 5 minutes at 350°F then cool.

10. Immediately the ice cream maker stops freezing, pour in the toasted almonds. Scoop ice cream into containers then freeze until ready to eat.

Chocolaty Flavored Hazelnut Ice Cream

Enjoy the combined taste of chocolate, cocoa and hazelnut in this ice cream. Yummy!

Preparation time: 30 minutes (plus 4 hours freezing time)

Cooking time: 20 minutes

Servings: 4 cups

Ingredients:

2 oz. bittersweet chocolate, diced

2 tbsp dark cocoa powder

2 oz. (½ cup) natural shelled hazelnuts

3 cups half and half

4 egg yolks

¾ cup turbinado sugar

½ tsp kosher salt

1 tbsp tapioca starch

Directions:

1. Heat up your oven to 425°F. Spread the hazelnuts on a baking sheet then roast for about 10 minutes until it turns dark. Slightly cool then rub off the skin with a clean kitchen towel; throw the skins away. Use a meat mallet or a rolling pin to crush the nuts roughly then set aside.

2. Heat up the half and half and sugar in a saucepan over medium heat, beating to melt the sugar but do not boil the mixture. Stir in the cocoa powder until it blends in then add the diced chocolate. Cook while stirring for about 2 minutes until the chocolate dissolves then lower heat to low.

3. In a small bowl, combine the egg yolks, tapioca starch and salt, then beat everything together. Add a cup of hot chocolate mixture; continue whisking to prevent the yolks from curdling.

4. Pour the chocolate-yolk mixture back into the saucepan then cook for 5 minutes, stirring frequently until it becomes a bit thick enough to coat the back of the spoon. Pass the mixture through a strainer then cool.

5. Chill the strained mixture in an ice bath. You may prepare this cream a day before then refrigerate.

6. Once chilled, pour the mixture into your ice cream maker then churn for 20 to 25 minutes until it becomes semi-firm. Add the hazelnuts and stir.

7. When ready, scoop the ice cream into a quart-size container then freeze for at least 4 hours or overnight before serving.

Peanut Butter Chocolate Ice Cream

Preparation time: 30 minutes

Cooking time: 7 minutes

Servings: 8

Ingredients:

4 tbsp cocoa powder

2 oz. semisweet chocolate

½ cup peanut butter, all-natural and 100% ground

1½ cups of milk

1 cup whipping cream

2 eggs, whisked slightly

2/3 cup sugar

1 tsp pure vanilla extract

Directions:

1. Dissolve the chocolate over low heat.

2. Stir in the cocoa powder and milk slowly while still heating.

3. In a bowl, whisk the sugar into the eggs.

4. Stir the hot chocolate-milk custard into the whisked eggs.

5. Pour in the cream and vanilla extract then cool.

6. Stir 1 cup of the cream mixture into the peanut butter, mix well then stir this mixture into the remaining cream mixture.

7. Pour the mixture into your ice cream maker then churn according to the manufacturer's directions.

Raspberry Chocolaty Ice Cream

Preparation time: 1 hour

Cooking time: 10 minutes

Servings: 3 cups

Ingredients:

2 cups fresh raspberries, thawed if frozen

5 tbsp cocoa powder, unsweetened and Dutch processed

1½ cups heavy cream

2/3 cup sugar

Directions:

1. In a large saucepan, beat the cream, sugar and cocoa powder together then heat, whisking constantly until it fully boils. Remove the mixture from heat then add the raspberries. Cover then let it sit for 10 minutes.

2. Pour the mixture in a blender then process until pureed. Pass the mixture through a fine strainer to remove the seeds.

3. Refrigerate the mixture until chilled then churn in your ice cream maker according to the manufacturer's instructions.

Peppermint Flavored Chocolate Ice Cream

Preparation time: 40 minutes (plus 4 hours freezing and overnight chilling)

Cooking time: 10 minutes

Servings: 8 (½ cup each)

Ingredients:

1/3 cup cocoa powder, unsweetened

2 oz. peppermint, roughly chopped

1 cup whipping cream

½ cup condensed milk, sweetened

½ cup granulated sugar

1½ cups of milk

1 tsp vanilla

Directions:

1. Combine cocoa powder, milk, sugar and condensed milk in a medium saucepan. Cook, stirring frequently over medium heat until it boils a bit. Lower the heat then simmer for 5 minutes, stirring frequently.

2. Pour the mixture into a storage container then stir in the diced peppermint, cover then refrigerate overnight.

3. Pass the chocolate mixture through a fine mesh strainer then throw away the solids. Stir in the whipping cream and vanilla.

4. Once chilled, churn the cream mixture in your 2-quart ice cream maker according to the manufacturer's instructions.

5. When ready, scoop the ice cream into an airtight storage container then freeze for 4 hours before serving.

GELATO RECIPES

Classic Creamy Gelato

Preparation time: 30 minutes (plus chilling and freezing time)

Cooking time: 10 minutes

Servings: 4 cups

Ingredients:

1 cup heavy cream

2 cups milk

½ cup sugar

4 egg yolks

Directions:

1. Mix the milk and cream together in a medium saucepan then warm over until it foams around the edges then remove from heat.

2. Whisk the egg yolks and sugar together in a large bowl until it becomes frothy. Pour the warm milk slowly into the yolk mixture, whisking frequently.

3. Pour the mixture back into the saucepan then cook over medium heat, using a wooden spoon to stir until it becomes sticky a bit and coats the back of the spoon. Remove the mixture from heat as soon as little egg lumps start to show.

4. Strain the mixture through a fine strainer into a clean bowl, cover then refrigerate for some hours or overnight until completely chilled.

5. Once chilled, pour the cream into your ice cream maker then churn according to the manufacturer's directions.

6. When done, scoop the ice cream into an airtight container then freeze until hard. If the gelato is very hard, refrigerate until you get your desired consistency.

Vanilla Flavored Gelato

Preparation time: 45 minutes

Cooking time: 15 minutes

Servings: 6 to 8

Ingredients:

2¼ cups whole milk

¾ cup heavy cream

1 vanilla bean, split lengthwise

¾ cup sugar

2 tbsp cornstarch

1 egg yolk

Directions:

1. Combine the cream, 1¼ cups of the milk and vanilla bean in a heavy-bottomed medium saucepan then heat over medium heat until it starts to boil and bubbles begins to appear around the edge of the pan.

2. In the mean time, combine the remaining cup of milk, cornstarch and sugar in a small bowl then stir until it blends well. Remove the saucepan with milk mixture from heat then add cornstarch mixture and stir. Put the pan back to the heat then cook, stirring constantly for 8 to 10 minutes until the sugar melts and a bit thick. Remove the saucepan from heat.

3. In a medium bowl, whisk the egg yolk until a bit thickened. Add 1 cup of the hot milk mixture into the whisked yolk, beating frequently then pour the mixture slowly back into the saucepan containing the hot milk mixture then stir with a wooden spoon.

4. Let the mixture sit to cool, stirring frequently then cover with plastic lid. Refrigerate overnight; take out the vanilla bean then throw it away.

5. Once chilled, churn the cream in your ice cream maker according to manufacturer's instructions.

Chocó Chocolaty Gelato

Preparation time: 40 minutes (plus 3 hours of freezing)

Cooking time: 10 minutes

Servings: 4 cups

Ingredients:

2 ounces bittersweet chocolate (not unsweetened)

1/3 cup of heavy cream

2¼ cups of whole milk

10 tablespoons superfine granulated sugar

1 cup of unsweetened cocoa powder

4 large egg yolks

Directions:

1. Chop the chocolate roughly. Bring the cream, milk and ½ of the sugar to a simmer in a 2-quart heavy saucepan, stir until the sugar melts. Remove the saucepan from heat then add the chocolate and cocoa powder, whisk until the chocolate dissolves and the custard smooth.

2. Get an ice bath ready in a large bowl. Use an electric mixer to whisk the egg yolks and the remaining sugar together in a bowl until it becomes pale and thick. Pour in the chocolate mixture in a gradual stream; whisk and pour into the pan.

3. Cook the mixture over medium-low heat, stir consistently until it reads 170°F by a thermometer but do not boil.

4. Strain the mixture through a fine strainer into a clean steel bowl then place in the prepared ice bath then cool; cover until chilled.

5. Once chilled, pour the mixture into your ice-cream maker and then process.

6. When done, scoop the ice cream into a sealable container then freeze for 1 to 3 hours until firm.

Flavored Hazelnut Gelato

Preparation time: 1 hour 30 minutes (plus freezing and cooling time)

Cooking time: 20 minutes

Servings: 4 cups

Ingredients:

1 cup hazelnuts

4 large egg yolks

2½ cups whole milk

1/3 cup heavy cream

¼ cup + 2 tbsp sugar

Directions:

1. Toast the hazelnuts then use a kitchen towel to rub off the skins then cool. Pour the toasted hazelnuts, ¼ cup of sugar and a pinch of salt in your blender then process until well diced.

2. Pour the pureed mixture into a 3-quart heavy saucepan then pour in the heavy milk and milk. Bring to just a simmer over medium heat, stirring once in a while then remove from the heat, leave it covered to steep for 1 hour.

3. Strain the mixture through a fine strainer into a clean bowl, press hard on the solids to bring out the liquid then throw away the solids.

4. Use an electric mixer to whisk the egg yolks and sugar together at medium speed for 2 to 3 minutes until it becomes pale and thick. Whisk in the milk mixture then transfer to a clean saucepan. Cook the mixture over medium-low heat, stirring consistently until it reads 175°F by an instant-read thermometer but do not boil.

5. Now, pass the mixture immediately through the cleaned sieve into a clean metal bowl, then chill on large bowl of ice bath, stirring irregularly. Chill the cream covered until cold.

6. Once chilled, pour the cream into your ice cream maker then churn according to the manufacturer's directions.

7. When done, scoop the ice cream into an airtight container then freeze to firm up.

Almond-Pistachio Gelato

This gelato is filled with nourishing flavors and tastes yummy when served with cookies.

Preparation time: 40 minutes (plus freezing and 3 hours chilling time)

Cooking time: 15 minutes

Servings: 6

Ingredients:

¾ cup no-salt-added shelled pistachios

1 teaspoon almond extract

¾ cup sugar

2 cups whole milk

5 large egg yolks

Green food coloring, 2 drops

For garnishing: diced no-salt-added pistachios

Directions:

1. Pour the pistachios and ¼ cup of sugar into a blender then process until finely ground.

2. In a heavy medium-size saucepan, combine the pistachio mixture, almond extract and milk then bring to a boil.

3. In a large bowl, beat the egg yolks and ½ cup of sugar together until well blended. Whisk in the milk mixture slowly.

4. Pour the mixture back into the saucepan then cook, stirring over medium-low heat for 8 minutes until it becomes a bit thick and coats the back of a spoon but do not boil. Remove the mixture from heat then stir in the food coloring. Refrigerate for about 3 hours until chilled.

5. Once chilled, pour the cream into your ice cream maker then freeze according to manufacturer's directions.

6. When done, spoon the ice cream into an airtight container, cover then freeze. When ready to eat scoop ice cream into bowls or glasses then top with diced pistachios.

Note: This ice cream can be prepared a week ahead and frozen.

Chocolaty Gelato

Lemon Flavored Gelato

Preparation time: 30 minutes (plus chilling and 2 hours freezing time)

Cooking time: 10 minutes

Servings: 8

Ingredients:

¾ cup lemon juice

3 tbsp minced lemon peel

1 cup milk

2 cups heavy whipping cream

5 egg yolks, lightly whisked

1 cup sugar

Directions:

1. Heat up the milk in a small heavy saucepan to 175°F then stir in the sugar until it melts. Stir in little quantity of the hot milk mixture into the whisked egg yolks. Pour everything back into the saucepan, whisking consistently.

2. Add the minced lemon peel then cook over low heat until it becomes a bit thick, enough to coat the back of a metal spoon and when it registers 160°F by a thermometer. Stir consistently but do not let it boil.

3. Remove the mixture from heat immediately then stir in the cream and lemon juice. Transfer the mixture to a bowl then cover with a plastic wrap, touching the surface of the mixture. Chill in the refrigerator for some hours or overnight.

4. Once chilled, pour the mixture into the cylinder of your ice cream maker about 2/3 full then churn according to the manufacturer's instructions.

5. Chill the remaining cream in the refrigerator until you are ready to freeze.

6. When ready, scoop the ice cream into freezer containers creating a headspace for expansion then freeze for 2 to 4 hours or until hard. Repeat this process with the remaining mixture.

Yummy Amarena Gelato

Preparation time: 30 minutes (5 hours freezing time)

Cooking time: 0 minute

Servings: 6 to 8

Ingredients:

3 tbsp diced amarena cherries

2 tbsp amarena syrup

2 cups whipping cream (or double cream)

14 oz. condensed milk

2 tsp vanilla extract

3 tbsp Crème de Cassis (or desired flavor)

Directions:

1. Beat the heavy cream with the condensed milk and vanilla essence until soft peaks appear but do not overbeat.

2. Whisk in the crème de cassis.

3. Pour the mixture into your ice cream maker then churn for 10 to 15 minutes.

4. Swirl in the diced cherries gradually.

5. When done, spoon the ice cream into containers then freeze for 5 to 7 hours to harden.

6. Sprinkle syrup over the ice cream before serving.

Yummy Tiramisu Gelato

Preparation time: 30 minutes (plus 6 hours of cooling and freezing)

Cooking time: 12 minutes

Servings: 10

Ingredients:

½ cup bittersweet chocolate, shaved

4 cups milk

1 tbsp vanilla bean puree

6 egg yolks

1¼ cups sugar

2 cups mascarpone cheese

1 tbsp instant coffee granules (or instant espresso)

¼ cup coffee liqueur

For garnishing; cocoa powder

Directions:

1. In a heavy saucepan, combine the milk and vanilla then bring to just a boil over medium heat.

2. In a bowl, beat the egg yolks and sugar together until well blended.

3. Whisk the hot milk mixture into the yolk mixture slowly, beating consistently. Pour the mixture back into the saucepan then cook on moderate-low heat for 7 minutes or until the batter slightly coats the back of a spoon. Stir consistently but do not boil then remove the mixture from heat.

4. Gradually add cheese the mix properly. Cover and refrigerate for 2 hours or until completely cooled then stir in the espresso granules.

5. Once chilled, pour the mixture into your ice cream maker then churn according to the manufacturer's instructions. After 20 minutes, stir in the chocolate and liqueur the freeze in containers for 4 hours before serving.

6. When ready to serve, sprinkle each gelato servings with cocoa powder. Enjoy!

Tasty Zabaglione Gelato

Preparation time: 40 minutes

Cooking time: 5 minutes

Servings: 4 cups

Ingredients:

2 cups heavy cream

8 large egg yolks

¾ cup marsala wine

½ cup sugar

Pinch of salt

Directions:

1. In a large mixing bowl, combine the egg yolks, marsala, sugar and salt. Pour water into a large saucepan then bring to a boil and turn off the heat. Place the bowl containing the mixture over the saucepan with hot water then whisk actively for 3 to 5 minutes or until it becomes thick, hot and doubles in size.

2. Remove the bowl from heat then place in a prepared ice bath. Whisk continuously until the zabaglione is cold.

3. Whip the cream until soft peaks starts to appear then stir into the chilled mixture.

4. Now, pour the custard into your ice-cream maker then freeze according to the manufacturer's directions.

5. When done, transfer to plastic containers.

Chocolate Creamy Stracciatella Gelato

Preparation time: 30 minutes (2 hours of cooling)

Cooking time: 10 minutes

Servings: 6

Ingredients:

2 cups whole milk

1/3 cup bittersweet chocolate chips

1 vanilla bean, split lengthwise

½ cup heavy whipping cream, chilled

¾ cup sugar

2 tsp vegetable oil

5 large egg yolks

Pinch of kosher salt

Directions:

1. Pour the milk into a medium-size saucepan then scrape in the vanilla bean seeds, bean and then simmer, beating frequently. In a medium bowl, beat the yolks, sugar and salt together for about a minute or until well combined.

2. Whisk the hot milk mixture slowly into the yolk mixture then pour into the saucepan. Stir and cook over medium-low heat for about 5 minutes or until it starts to thickens and reads 170°F to 175°F by a thermometer but do not boil.

3. Pass the custard through a fine strainer into a clean medium-size bowl then stir in the cream. Refrigerate the mixture for at least 2 hours until cold.

4. In a small saucepan, heat the chocolate and oil over low heat, stirring until it dissolves and then cool.

5. Now, pour the cream into your ice cream maker then churn according to the manufacturer's directions.

6. Reserve 1 tsp of the dissolve chocolate then pour the remaining mixture slowly into the ice cream when it's about 30 seconds before churning time ends, the chocolate will form small chips.

7. When ready, spoon into a bowl then sprinkle the reserved chocolate over the gelato in zigzag lines. Serve immediately.

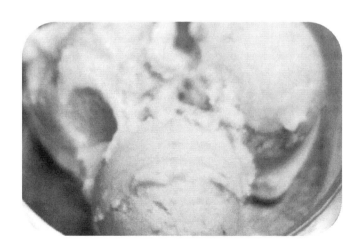

Honey-Beet Frozen Yogurt

Preparation time: 40 minutes (plus 2 hours chilling time)

Cooking time: 45 minutes

Servings: 4 cups

Ingredients:

3 cups of Greek yogurt, 2%

5 beets

½ cup of honey

1 teaspoon olive oil

Sprinkle of salt

Directions:

1. Preheat your oven to 400°F.

2. Use an aluminum foil to wrap the beets including the skin then sprinkle 1 tsp of olive oil and salt.

3. Roast the beets for 45 minutes or until the beets feel soft when dipped with fork and then cool slightly so you can easily remove the peel.

4. Blend the beets until smooth then refrigerate for at least 2 hours.

5. Mix the yoghurt, honey and beet paste in a bowl until well blended.

6. Pour the mixture into the frozen sleeve of your ice cream maker then churn for about 30 minutes until you get the soft serve consistency.

7. Freeze for later use or serve immediately.

Cherry Chocolaty Frozen Yogurt

Preparation time: 6 hours 15 minutes (includes cooling and churning time)

Cooking time: 5 minutes

Servings: 4 cups

Ingredients:

1/3 cup cocoa powder

4 cups zero-fat plain yogurt

1½ cups fresh cherries, pitted and halved

1 cup non-fat milk

2/3 cup sugar

1½ teaspoons vanilla extract

Directions:

1. Place a thick paper towel-lined mesh strainer (a large one) over a large, deep mixing bowl.

2. Pour the yogurt into the lined strainer then cover with plastic wrap and allow it strain in the refrigerator for at least 6 hours or overnight (this will stop the frozen yogurt from being very icy.)

3. In a small saucepan, combine the milk, vanilla and sugar then heat up over medium-low heat, warm it a bit enough to melt the sugar then set aside to cool.

4. Take out the straining yogurt from the refrigerator then pour the strained liquid gently into a large mixing bowl then stir in the cocoa powder.

5. Pour the cooled milk mixture into the mixing bowl containing the yogurt then stir until well combined and extremely smooth. Stir in the cherries, cover with plastic then refrigerate for at least 4 hours or preferably overnight.

6. Once chilled, Pour the mixture into your ice-cream maker then churn according to the machine's directions.

7. Serve immediately if you want a soft serve or freeze in an air tight container to harden.

8. When ready to eat, let it sit for a while to soften before serving.

Chocolate Hazelnut Frozen Yogurt

Make delicious hazelnut frozen yogurt in the comfort of your home with just the ingredients you can find in your kitchen.

Preparation time: 40 minutes (plus 30 minutes freezing time)

Cooking time: 0 minute

Servings: 4

Ingredients:

2 cups yogurt (any desired choice)

2/3 cup chocolate hazelnut butter (or Healthy Nutella)

1½ teaspoons pure vanilla extract, (no need for vanilla yogurt)

¼ teaspoon salt, or less

¼ cup cocoa powder or cacao

Pinch of pure stevia (or 1/3 cup of sugar or preferred sweetener)

1 cup milk (any desired choice but lower to 2/3 cup if you want to use a liquid sweetener)

Chocolate chips (optional)

Directions:

1. Process all the ingredients except the chocolate chips in your blender the stir vigorously by hand if possible until very smooth.

2. Pour the mixture into your ice cream maker then churn according to the machine's instructions. When done, turn off the machine then fold in chips, if desired.

3. Serve immediately as soft-serve, or freeze 30 minutes in an airtight container to harden.

Note that the yoghurt used is sweetened so you may add more sugar if you are using unsweetened.

Pistachio Almond Frozen Yogurt

Preparation time: 40 minutes (plus 2 hours freezing time)

Cooking time: 0 minute

Servings: 2

Ingredients:

¾ cup no-fat plain Greek yogurt

1 medium banana, chopped into chunks and frozen

½ cup raw spinach (or 1 small nugget frozen spinach)

¼ 1 medium avocado, (or 1 oz.)

2 tbsp pure honey or 2 packets of stevia

¼ tsp pure almond extract (or more to taste)

1/8 tsp xanthan gum (optional)

1 tbsp shelled pistachios + more for garnishing

4 - 5 ice cubes

Directions:

1. Pour the yogurt, avocado, banana, almond extract, spinach, stevia, pistachio and xanthan gum into your blender then process by pulsing and grinding a few times.

2. Once the mixture is well blended, pour it into a loaf pan then sprinkle pistachios over it.

3. Pour the mixture into your ice cream maker then churn according to the manufacturer's directions.

4. Freeze the yogurt for 2 to 3 hours until hard enough to scoop. Enjoy!

All-Natural Mango Frozen Yogurt

Enjoy cream mango frozen yogurt prepared with natural ingredients. It's easy to make and yummy.

Preparation time: 40 minutes (plus chilling time)

Cooking time: 15 minutes

Servings: 4 cups

Ingredients:

16 oz. fresh mango chunks, or frozen

2/3 cup honey

2 cups full-fat yogurt, chilled

1 small lime, juiced

1/8 tsp salt

Directions:

1. Combine the fresh or frozen mango, lime juice, honey and salt in a medium-size saucepan then bring to a soft boil over medium heat. Lower the heat to get a simmer then cook, stirring often for 15 minutes.

2. Remove the mango mixture from heat then cool for a couple of minutes. Pour the mixture into a blender then puree until very smooth.

3. Pour the pureed mixture into a large bowl then refrigerate for some hours or overnight until completely chilled. You may speed up the process by freezing for 45 minutes, stirring every 15 minutes.

4. Combine the chilled yogurt and the chilled mango mixture, then pour into your ice cream maker and churn according to the machine's directions.

5. Serve immediately for a soft serve texture or pour into a freezer-safe container then freeze for some hours until hard enough to scoop.

Vanilla Crème Frozen Yogurt

Preparation time: 25 minutes

Cooking time: 0 minutes

Servings: 4

Ingredients:

2 tsp vanilla extract

3 cups reduced-fat Greek yogurt (or non-fat plain yogurt)

¼ cup honey (or ½ cup maple syrup or agave nectar)

¼ tsp salt

Directions:

1. In a medium or large bowl, combine all the ingredients then stir. Pour the mixture into your ice cream maker then freeze for about 20 to 25 minutes or according to the manufacturer's instructions until you get a soft-serve texture.

2. To store or get a firm frozen yogurt, pour the yogurt into an airtight container then freeze. Cover the surface of the yogurt with a wax paper if storing for more than a day, then place a lid over it; this will hinder the formation of ice crystals on the surface.

Vegan Mint Chocó Frozen Yogurt

Preparation time: 40 minutes

Cooking time: 0 minute

Servings: 3

Ingredients:

½ cup fresh mint leaves (or ¼ teaspoon mint extract)

½ cup fresh spinach (or 2 drops of green food coloring)

1/3 cup almond milk

2 cups Greek yogurt (or coconut yogurt or vegan soy)

¼ cup honey/agave syrup (or ½ substituted with stevia powder)

1 chocolate protein bar, chopped (or homemade brownies, 2 servings)

1 large scoop of vanilla/chocolate/mint or desired flavored protein powder

For the brownie:

Vegan brownie oatmeal breakfast cookies

Dark chocolate protein bars, flourless and gluten-free (or your preferred protein bar)

Gluten-free fudge brownies

Directions:

1. Freeze the mixing bowl piece before making the frozen yogurt.

2. Pour the mint leaves, fresh spinach and 1/3 cup of almond milk into your blender then process until smooth. Pass the mixture through a fine strainer into a clean medium-size bowl, pressing on the solid to extract juice. Note that if you are using food coloring and mint extract, simply add them to the bowl, no need for blending.

3. Pour the Greek yogurt, protein powder and honey or agave into the bowl containing the mint mixture then stir everything together until well blended.

4. Pour the mixture into the prepared mixing bowl in your ice cream mixer then churn on slow setting for about 10 to 20 minutes to achieve a soft serve consistency.

5. When done, add the chopped protein bar or brownie, then stir with a rubber spatula to combine.

6. Serve immediately for soft-serve or freeze in individual serving portions for later. When ready to eat, thaw in the microwave for 10 to 30 seconds and eat.

Cooking tip: Unsweetened non-fat or plain Greek yogurt and almond milk was used in this recipe but whole or low fat Greek yogurt will give you a creamier consistency. You may use the sweetened version and omit the sweeteners if desired.

Chocolaty Frozen Yogurt

Preparation time: 30 minutes

Cooking time: 0 minute

Servings: 3 to 4

Ingredients:

½ cup chocolate powder

½ cup almond milk (or preferred milk)

2 cups plain or vanilla yogurt (use Greek but not lighter versions)

1 tsp vanilla extract

2 tsp truvia (or preferred sweetener substitute and add to taste)

Directions:

1. Puree all the ingredients in your blender. Truvia is more concentrated than regular sugar so adjust the quantity of sweetener you use, if you are substituting truvia for another sweetener.

2. Pour the mixture into your already prepared ice cream maker then churn for about 25 minutes or according to the manufacturer's instructions.

3. Serve immediately or scoop the yogurt into an airtight container then freeze to firm up, if desired. You may as well serve straight from the ice cream maker.

Raspberry Flavored Frozen Yogurt

Preparation time: 30 minutes (plus 1 hour cooling time)

Cooking time: 0 minute

Servings: 6

Ingredients:

10.6 oz. frozen raspberries

1½ cups plain non-fat Greek yogurt

1/3 cup honey

Directions:

1. Pour all the ingredients into your blender then puree for 4 to 5 minutes or until creamy and smooth.

2. Pour the mixture into a large bowl then refrigerate for 1 hour.

3. Once chilled, transfer the mixture to your ice cream maker then churn according to the manufacturer's directions.

4. Scoop the yogurt into an airtight container then freeze until you are ready to serve. Enjoy!

Rosehip-Strawberry Frozen Yogurt

Preparation time: 40 minutes

Cooking time: 5 minutes

Servings: 3 cups

Ingredients:

3 cups strawberries, fresh or frozen

2 tbsp rosehips (or 2 rosehip tea bags)

3 cups plain non-fat Greek yogurt

1½ cups whole-fat coconut milk (or any preferred milk)

½ cup honey

1 tsp vanilla bean

Directions:

1. In a small saucepan, heat up the milk and honey over low heat until it starts to steam and simmer but do not boil the milk. Add in the vanilla bean seeds and rosehips/tea bags, cover then allow it steep for 10 minutes.

2. Pass the mixture through a fine strainer into a clean bowl then throw away the vanilla bean and rosehips. Pour the strained mixture into your blender, add 2 cups of strawberries then process until smooth.

3. Pour in the Greek yogurt then process again until well mixed.

4. Dice the remaining cup of strawberries then pour it into the blender; process until the strawberries are evenly combined but not pureed. Note that if you don't want strawberry chunks in your yogurt, process all the strawberries at once when the milk is added.

5. Refrigerate the mixture until chilled.

6. Once chilled, freeze the mixture in your ice cream maker according to the manufacturer's instructions.

7. Serve as soft serve or freeze in an airtight container to harden until you are ready to eat.

Cooking tip: You may substitute honey for sugar. Add more sugar or honey for a sweeter yogurt.

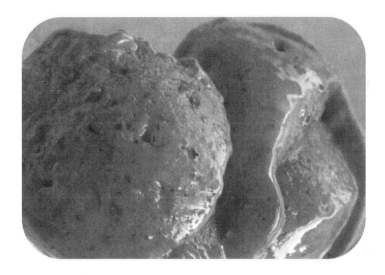

SHERBET RECIPES

Lemon Flavored Sherbet

Preparation time: 4 hours

Cooking time: 0 minute

Servings: 4 cups

Ingredients:

½ cup lemon juice powder

¾ cup granulated sugar

2 lemons, juiced and chilled (or ½ cup fresh lemon juice)

2 cups chilled whole milk

1 tbsp cornstarch (optional, for smoother texture)

Directions:

1. Pour the lemon juice powder and sugar into your blender then process 8 to 10 times to blend well. Note that the lemon juice powder should be blended with sugar first because it doesn't dissolve in liquid easily.

2. Pour the milk, chilled lemon juice and cornstarch into your blender then pulse for 30 seconds to mix well. You may also whisk everything together in a bowl method until well combined.

3. Pour the mixture into your ice cream maker then churn according to the machine's instructions.

Raspberry Cinnamon Sherbet

Preparation time: 1 hour 10 minutes

Cooking time: 5 minutes

Servings: 4

Ingredients:

2 cups wild raspberries

1/8 tsp ground cinnamon

¼ cup white sugar

¼ tsp lemon juice

1½ cups of milk

Directions:

1. In a small saucepan, heat up the raspberries and sugar over low heat, stir for about 5 minutes or until the sugar melts. Strain the mixture through a fine strainer into a clean bowl then throw away the seeds.

2. Whisk lemon juice, cinnamon and milk into the raspberry mixture then chill for about an hour or until cold.

3. Pour the chilled mixture into your ice cream maker then freeze according to manufacturer's directions.

Vanilla Strawberry Mint Sherbet

Preparation time: 1 hour 25 minutes

Cooking time: 0 minute

Servings: 4

Ingredients:

2 cups fresh strawberries (or 16 oz. frozen strawberries, thawed)

1 tsp vanilla extract

2 cups buttermilk

1 cup sugar

Fresh mint sprigs, for garnish

Directions:

1. Pulse the strawberries in your blender for 30 seconds or until smooth then stop to scrape down the sides.

2. Strain the strawberry paste through a fine strainer into a large bowl, pressing the solids with the back of a spoon to extract liquid then throw away the solids. Pour the vanilla, buttermilk and sugar into the strawberry puree then stir properly until well combined. Cover then refrigerate for 1 hour.

3. Once chilled, pour the mixture into the freezer container of your 1½ quart electric ice-cream maker then churn according to maker's directions. Note that the time and instructions may vary.

4. When done, garnish your sherbet, if desired then serve.

Creamy Lime Cherry Sherbet

Preparation time: 30 minutes

Cooking time: 0 minute

Servings: 8 cups

Ingredients:

4 cups milk

6 oz. frozen limeade concentrate, thawed

3 oz. cherry gelatin

2 cups half and half

1 cup boiling water

1¼ cups sugar

Dash of salt

8 drops of green food coloring (opt)

Directions:

1. Melt the gelatin in a large bowl with water. Add the limeade, sugar and salt then mix until the sugar completely dissolves. Pour in the remaining ingredients then incorporate.

2. Pour the mixture into your ice cream maker then churn according to the manufacturer's instructions.

Sweet Lime Sherbet

Preparation time: 1 hour 25 minutes

Cooking time: 10 minutes

Servings: 4

Ingredients:

2/3 cup lime juice

1 cup granulated sugar

1 tbsp lime zest

2 cups whole milk, chilled

1 cup water

2 drops of green food coloring (opt)

Directions:

1. In a small saucepan, heat up the granulated sugar and water, stirring often until the sugar completely melts. This sugar syrup will help make your sherbet have a smooth consistency.

2. Remove the sugar syrup from heat then whisk in the lime zest and juice then refrigerate until completely cold.

3. Once chilled, stir in the milk and food coloring.

4. Pour the mixture into your ice cream maker then freeze according to the manufacturer's instructions.

5. When done, transfer the sherbet to an air-tight plastic container then freeze to firm up.

6. Garnish with fresh lime slice then serve.

Cooking tip: You may omit the food coloring but note that you will end up with a bright white sherbet. A little drop of food coloring will help identify the flavor at a glance.

Chocolate Almond Sherbet

Preparation time: 40 minutes

Cooking time: 0 minute

Servings: 4

Ingredients:

¾ cup cocoa powder, unsweetened

2 tbsp almond flavored liqueur (amaretto)

1 cup sugar

1½ cups of water

Directions:

1. Whisk the cocoa, amaretto, sugar and water together in a medium-size bowl until very smooth.

2. Pour the mixture into the freezer container of your ice cream maker then churn according to the manufacturer's directions.

Avocado-Lime Cilantro Sherbet

Preparation time: 40 minutes (plus 3 hours chilling and freezing time)

Cooking time: 10 minutes

Servings: 4 cups

Ingredients:

2 firm-ripe avocados, roughly diced (about 1 lb.)

1 cup fresh cilantro leaves, packed

1 tbsp fresh lime juice

1 cup whole milk

2/3 cup sugar

2/3 cup water

Directions:

1. In a small saucepan, bring water and sugar to a boil, stirring until the sugar completely melts. Remove the sugar syrup from heat then add the cilantro. Allow it steep for 15 minutes then strain through a fine strainer into a bowl then throw away the solids. Refrigerate the liquid for about 15 minutes until chilled.

2. Pulse the chopped avocados, lime juice and cilantro syrup in your food processor until very smooth. Pour the mixture into a bowl then stir in the milk. Cover then refrigerate for at least an hour to 2 hours or until chilled.

3. Chill a loaf pan in the freezer at least 10 minutes.

4. Pour the chilled mixture into your ice cream maker then churn according to manufacturer's instructions.

5. When done, transfer the sherbet to the chilled pan then cover with a plastic wrap then freeze for at least 2 hours or until firm.

Note: This sherbet can be frozen for up to 2 weeks ahead.

Creamy Ginger Grapefruit Sherbet

Preparation time: 50 minutes

Cooking time: 10 minutes

Servings: 4¼ cups

Ingredients:

1 cup buttermilk

¼ cup fresh ginger, peeled, grated and juiced

3 cups fresh ruby-red grapefruit juice, strained and divided

1 tbsp minced grapefruit peel

½ cup whipping cream

¾ cup sugar

¼ cup light corn syrup

Directions:

1. In a heavy medium-size saucepan, mix 1 of cup grapefruit juice, ginger with juices, sugar and grapefruit peel together then heat over medium-high heat until the sugar melts then bring to a boil. Remove the mixture from heat then cool for 30 minutes.

2. Stir the corn syrup into the mixture followed by the buttermilk. Whisk in the remaining 2 cups of juice then press the mixture through a fine strainer into a large bowl to extract enough juice then throw away the solids.

3. Pour the strained mixture into your ice cream maker then churn according to the manufacturer's directions.

4. Pour in the cream once the sherbet is softly set. Churn for another 5 minutes until it blends well.

5. Once done, pour the sherbet into a container, cover then freeze.

Apple-Lemon Sherbet

Preparation time: 50 minutes

Cooking time: 10 minutes

Servings: 4 cups

Ingredients:

5 lbs. Granny Smith apples

1 egg white

1 tsp lemon juice

½ cup sugar

¼ cup water

Directions:

1. In a small saucepan, measure the sugar and water then stir together and heat over low heat until the sugar melt.

2. In a bowl, beat the egg white until fluffy and light.

3. Slice the apples, remove the cores, chop into chunks then push the apple chunks through the juice extractor as you go.

4. When done, whisk the apple puree, egg white, sugar syrup and lemon juice together immediately. Do not worry if the egg white rises to the surface, it will blend well once the sherbet is frozen.

5. Pour the mixture into your ice cream maker then churn according to the maker's directions.

Creamy Vanilla Orange Sherbet

Preparation time: 1 hour 50 minutes

Cooking time: 0 minute

Servings: 4 cups

Ingredients:

2 – 3 lbs oranges, freshly squeezed (about 2 cups of freshly squeezed juice)

1½ tbsp finely minced orange zest

1½ cups whole milk, very chilled

1 tsp vanilla extract

7 oz. sugar

¼ tsp kosher salt

1 tbsp freshly squeezed lemon juice

Directions:

1. Pour all the ingredients except the milk into the bowl of your blender then pulse for about 1 minute or until the sugar dissolves.

2. Pour the mixture into a mixing bowl then stir in the milk. Cover the bowl then refrigerate for about an hour or until it gets to 40°F or lower.

3. Pour the chilled mixture into your ice cream maker then churn until you get a soft serve ice cream texture.

4. You may serve as soft serve if desired or pour the sherbet into an airtight container then freeze for about 3 hours to firm up.

ADULTS ICE CREAM
(E.G. ALCOHOLIC FLAVORS)

Vanilla Scotch Ice Cream

Preparation time: 1 hour 45 minutes (plus overnight chilling)

Cooking time: 15 minutes

Servings: 4 cups

Ingredients:

3 tbsp Highlands Scotch whisky

1 Mexican/Bourbon vanilla bean, split and scraped

1 tsp vanilla extract

2 cups cream

8 egg yolks

1 cup whole milk

¾ cup sugar

1 tsp kosher salt, or to taste

Directions:

1. Bring the milk and cream to just a simmer in a heavy saucepan, stir in the vanilla bean and seeds, cover then allow it steep for 1 hour. Remove the bean then wash away the dairy then set it aside to dry. You may add spent bean to a jar of sugar to make vanilla sugar.

2. In a bowl, beat the egg yolks and sugar together until light and well mixed. Pour the yolk mixture gradually into the dairy mixture then whisk to mix well. Cook the mixture on low heat, beating often until it becomes thick enough to coat the back of a spoon; it should leave a fine line when swiped with a finger.

3. Pass the mixture through a fine strainer into an airtight container then stir in the scotch and vanilla. Add salt to taste then refrigerate overnight.

4. Once chilled, pour the custard into your ice cream maker then freeze according to the manufacturer's directions.

5. Serve at once as soft-serve or freeze for 2 to 3 hours to harden.

Bourbon Creamy Mint Ice Cream

Preparation time: 1 hour 35 minutes (plus overnight chilling)

Cooking time: 25 minutes

Servings: 4 cups

Ingredients:

¼ cup of bourbon

2 oz. mint leaves, (spearmint)

1½ cups of milk

6 egg yolks

1½ cups of cream

¾ cup of sugar

¼ tsp kosher salt

1 tsp vanilla extract

Directions:

1. Use a wooden spoon to bruise the mint leaves to release flavors and essential oils then transfer them to a saucepan. Add milk and ¾ cup of cream then simmer. Remove the mixture from heat, cover then let it steep for 30 minutes

2. Place a bowl containing the remaining cream on a large bowl filled with ice water. Place a fine strainer over the bowl with cream. Beat the egg yolks together in another bowl.

3. Strain the steeped cream mixture through a fine strainer then discard the mint leaves. Pour the cream-milk mixture back into the saucepan then add the sugar and salt. Heat up the mixture over medium heat until steaming but not boiling.

4. Pour some of the hot milk mixture slowly into the egg yolk then beat consistently until the yolks are tempered by the hot milk but do not allow it cook. Transfer the mixture back into the saucepan.

5. Set over medium heat, stirring consistently with a wooden spoon then scrape the bottom of the pan while you stir. Cook the custard for 3 to 10 minutes until it becomes thick enough to coat the back of a spoon and not runny.

6. Once thick, pass the mixture through a fine mesh sieve into the chilled bowl of cream. Stir in the vanilla and bourbon, cover then refrigerate for 6 hours or overnight until very cold.

7. Once chilled, pour the custard into your ice cream maker then churn according to the manufacturer's directions.

8. The ice cream has a soft-serve texture after churning but needs to be hardened up a little. Scoop the ice cream into an airtight container then freeze for some hours to firm up before serving.

Sauvignon Brandy Ice Cream

Preparation time: 30 minutes (plus 4 hours freezing time and overnight chilling)

Cooking time: 40 minutes

Servings: 4 cups

Ingredients:

½ tsp coriander seed

2 cups Cabernet Sauvignon

6 allspice berries

4 cardamom pods, mashed slightly

2 blades mace

¼ inch cinnamon stick

1 star anise star

1 orange

1 tbsp brandy

6 egg yolks

¾ cup sugar

2 cups heavy cream

1 cup whole milk

½ tsp kosher salt

Directions:

1. Toast the spices in a dry skillet over high heat for about 30 seconds, stirring often until it becomes aromatic.

2. Bring the wine and spices to a simmer in a medium non-reactive saucepan over medium heat. Squeeze out juice from 1 orange through a strainer then remove the seeds. Pour the orange juice into the pan then cook, stirring often until the wine becomes thick, bubbly and measures about ¼ cup. Strain the spices and orange mixture then set aside to cool.

3. Get another medium saucepan then beat the egg yolks and sugar together until well blended and a bit thickened. Stir in the milk and cream until it blends well then pour in the reduced wine. Cook over medium heat until the mixture is thick enough to coat a spoon and leaves a clean line when swiped across with a finger.

4. Strain the custard through a strainer into an airtight container then stir in the brandy and salt to taste then refrigerate overnight.

5. On the next day, pour the chilled custard into your ice cream maker then churn according to manufacturer's directions.

6. When done, freeze the ice cream for at least 4 hour to firm up before serving.

Vanilla Rum Ice Cream

Preparation time: 30 minutes (plus 4 hours chilling and freezing time)

Cooking time: 15 minutes

Servings: 6 cups

Ingredients:

3 tbsp dark rum

1 tsp vanilla

1 cup whole milk

¼ tsp salt

7 large egg yolks

¾ cup sugar

2 cups heavy cream, chilled

¼ tsp freshly grated nutmeg

Freshly grated nutmeg, for garnishing

Directions:

1. In a 2 to 3qt heavy saucepan, bring the milk and salt to a boil over medium heat then remove the pan from heat.

2. In a bowl, beat the yolks and sugar together then add ¼ cup of the hot milk gradually, whisking. Pour the yolk mixture in a slow stream into the remaining milk in the pan. Whisk, then cook over low heat for 3 to 5 minutes, stirring often with a wooden spoon until it thickens a bit and it registers 175°F on thermometer.

3. Now, pass the mixture through a fine strainer into a clean bowl then stir in the rum, cream, nutmeg and vanilla then cover and refrigerate for at least 2 hours or until chilled.

4. When chilled, pour the custard into your ice cream maker then churn according to the manufacturer's directions.

5. When done, freeze in an airtight container for at least 2 hours to firm up.

6. Refrigerate the ice cream for about 20 minutes to soften before serving.

Note: The custard can be refrigerated for up to a day. The ice cream can be made a week ahead.

Caramel Ale Ice Cream

Preparation time: 30 minutes (plus overnight cooling and 2 hours freezing time)

Cooking time: 30 minutes

Servings: 4

Ingredients:

8 oz. pale ale

4 tbsp no-salt-added butter, sliced into small pieces

1½ cups sugar

2 tbsp water

2 cups heavy cream

1 cup whole milk

6 egg yolks

1 tsp kosher salt, to taste

Directions:

1. Heat up sugar with 2 tbsp of water in a deep heavy saucepan over high heat. Allow the sugar dissolve, bubble then caramelize without distributing

until it becomes rich, dark amber then rotate the pan to prevent hot spots. Allow the sugar smoke for 3 seconds, then stir in the butter quickly; reduce the heat to low.

2. Once the butter completely blends in, stir in the milk and cream gradually then cook until the sugar steams and bubbles. Stir the mixture on low heat if the sugar seizes so it melts completely into dairy.

3. Beat the egg yolk in a large bowl until well mixed. Pour in about 2/3 cup of the dairy mixture, a ladle at a time then whisk consistently. Now, whisk the mixture back into the saucepan then cook on low heat, stirring often until it becomes thick enough to coat the back of a spoon and leaves a fine line when swiped with a finger.

4. Remove the custard from heat then whisk in the beer, add salt to taste. Note that the custard has enough salt when it has a distinctly sharp flavor and not a burnt sweetness.

5. Pass the custard through a fine strainer into a container then refrigerate overnight.

6. On the next day, pour the chilled custard into your ice cream maker then churn according to manufacturer's directions.

7. When done, freeze the ice cream for at least 2 hours to harden.

Choco whisky ice cream

Chocó Whisky Ice Cream

Preparation time: 1 hour 10 minutes

Cooking time: 15 minutes

Servings: 4 cups

Ingredients:

3 oz. diced semisweet chocolate

¼ cup whiskey

4 egg yolks

¼ cup mini chocolate chips

¼ cup sugar + ¼ cup

1½ cups heavy cream

1 vanilla bean split, seeds scraped

Directions:

1. In a medium bowl, beat the egg yolks, ¼ cup of sugar and whiskey together then set aside.

2. Beat the cream, ¼ cup of sugar, vanilla bean and seeds together in a large saucepan then bring to a simmer over low heat until the chocolate dissolves.

3. Stir the hot cream mixture slowly, a little at a time into the yolk mixture to temper the egg. Pour the egg yolk mixture back into the saucepan with cream immediately the egg yolk mixture is completely warmed then stir until thick then remove from heat.

4. Pass the custard through a fine strainer into a bowl placed over ice bath. Refrigerate for at least 45 minutes.

5. Once chilled, stir in the chocolate chips then pour into your ice cream maker then churn for 20 minutes until you get a soft-serve texture.

Creamy Vanilla Bourbon Ice Cream

Preparation time: 35 minutes (plus 5 hours cooling time)

Cooking time: 10 minutes

Servings: 4

Ingredients:

2 cups heavy whipping cream

1½ cups whole milk

½ cup bourbon

¼ cup sugar

2 tbsp vanilla extract

6 egg yolks

½ tsp sea salt

Directions:

1. In a large saucepan, mix the milk, cream, sugar and salt together then cook over a moderate heat, stirring often.

2. Pour the yolks in a heat-proof bowl then lightly beat. Once the cream mixture begins to steam and tiny bubbles appear along the edge of the pan, then whisk about a cup into the yolks, ¼ cup at a time. Increase the temperature of the eggs so the eggs don't curdle when adding it to the cream.

3. Whisk the eggs gradually into the cream mixture immediately the eggs are tempered, stirring consistently then cook over low heat for about 5 minutes or until it becomes thick enough to coat the back of a wooden spoon. Turn off the heat then stir in the bourbon and vanilla extract.

4. Pour the mixture into a large bowl, cover then refrigerate for about 5 hours or more. For a faster result, chill the custard by placing it over a bowl of ice water.

5. Once chilled, pour the custard into your ice cream maker then churn according to the manufacturer's directions. Note that the ice cream might still be runny even after 20 to 30 minutes of churning.

6. Freeze the ice cream for some hours or overnight to firm up.

Gin-Tonic Berry Ice Cream

Preparation time: 1 hour 50 minutes (plus 8 hours of freezing and cooling)

Cooking time: 15 minutes

Servings: 4 cups

Ingredients:

3 tbsp juniper berries

¼ cup London Dry Gin

2 cups whole milk, divided

3 tbsp cream cheese, softened

1¼ cups heavy cream, divided

½ cup sugar

2 tbsp corn syrup

1 tbsp + 1 tsp cornstarch

1/8 tsp salt

1/8 tsp ground quinine bark (optional)

Directions:

1. Grind the juniper berries roughly then mix with ½ cup of cream, 1½ cups of milk, corn syrup and sugar in a medium-size saucepan; warm over medium heat. Immediately it gets warm, cover then remove from heat and let it steep for an hour at room temperature.

2. In the mean time, pour ice water into a large bowl; combine 2 tbsp of milk and cornstarch in a small bowl. Beat the cream cheese and salt together in a medium bowl until smooth then place a fine strainer over the bowl then set it aside.

3. Once it completely steeps, pour the remaining milk and cream into the juniper soaked mixture then bring to a low boil over medium heat. Add the ground quinine bark then boil for about 4 minutes until it starts to thicken.

4. Remove the mixture from heat then turn off the heat. Whisk the cornstarch mixture gradually into the custard then bring to a boil over medium-high heat for a minute or until it becomes thick a bit.

5. Strain the hot milk mixture slowly through a fine strainer into the cream cheese then whisk until very smooth then stir in the gin. Place the bowl in the prepared ice water bath then let it sit for about 20 minutes, stirring often until chilled.

6. Refrigerate the mixture for at least 4 hours or overnight. Once chilled, pour the mixture into your ice cream maker then churn according to the maker's directions.

7. Cover the surface of the ice cream with a plastic or parchment to avoid ice crystals from forming then freeze for at least 4 hours until hard.

8. Serve ice cream with a squeeze of lime juice on top, if desired.

Rum-Pineapple Ice Cream

Preparation time: 1 hour 30 minutes (plus 5 hours chilling and freezing time)

Cooking time: 20 minutes

Servings: 7 Cups

Ingredients:

¾ cups dark rum

2 cups finely diced fresh pineapple

1 cup whole milk

3 cups whipping cream

½ cup pineapple juice

1 vanilla bean, split lengthwise

2¼ cups sugar

10 large egg yolks

Directions:

1. In a heavy big saucepan, mix the cream and milk together then scrape in the vanilla bean seeds and the bean itself. Bring to a simmer then remove from heat. Stir in ¾ cup of sugar and ¼ cup of rum.

2. In a large bowl, beat the yolks and ¾ cup of sugar together until it starts to thicken then whisk in the pineapple juice, followed by the hot cream mixture. Pour the mixture back into the saucepan then stir over medium-low heat for about 10 minutes or until it becomes thick enough to coat the back of a spoon and leaves a fine line when swiped with a finger but do not boil.

3. Pass the mixture through a fine strainer into a large bowl then chill for about 2 hours until cold.

4. In the meantime, combine ¾ cup of sugar, diced pineapple and ½ cup of rum in a medium-size bowl then let it sit for an hour. Bring the mixture to a boil then lower the heat and simmer for 3 minutes, stirring often. Drain the pineapple then cool.

5. Pour the mixture into your ice cream maker then churn according to the maker's directions until it starts to thicken.

6. Once the ice cream is semi-firm, add the pineapple then scoop into a container. Cover then freeze for about 3 hours until hard.

Irish Cream Ice Cream

Preparation time: 30 minutes (plus overnight freezing)

Cooking time: 0 minute

Servings: 4

Ingredients:

1 cup Irish cream liqueur

2 cups whole milk

1 cup heavy cream

½ cup ultrafine sugar

Directions:

1. Combine all the ingredients.

2. Freeze your preferred ice cream container.

3. Pour the mixture in your ice cream maker then churn according to the manufacturer's directions. The ice cream texture may still be runny after churning time due to the alcohol in it.

4. Once you finish churning, pour the ice cream into the chilled container.

5. Cover then freeze overnight.

Cooking tip: Use about ½ cup of Irish cream to get a firmer and mild ice cream.

Caramelized Brown Sugar Topping

Preparation time: 2 minutes

Cooking time: 5 minutes

Servings: 2 cups

Ingredients:

½ cup salted butter

¼ tsp salt

1 cup packed brown sugar

2/3 cup heavy whipping cream, unwhipped

2 – 4 tsp vanilla extract (optional)

Directions:

1. Dissolve the butter with salt in a small saucepan.

2. Stir in the brown sugar; whisking for about 2 minutes until well mixed and thick.

3. Stir in the whipping cream, whisking for another 2 minutes until it completely incorporates.

4. Stir in the vanilla (if using) until well combined.

Note: this topping will become thick when refrigerated.

Chocolate Vanilla Topping

Preparation time: 4 minutes

Cooking time: 7 minutes

Servings: 2 cups

Ingredients:

1/3 cup unsweetened cocoa powder

1 cup butter

12 oz. evaporated milk

3 cups white sugar

1 tsp vanilla extract

Directions:

1. In a saucepan, mix the cocoa, butter, sugar and evaporated milk together then heat over medium heat. Bring to a boil for 7 minutes then remove from heat. Now, stir in the vanilla.

2. Pour the hot mixture carefully into the blender then pulse for 2 to 4 minutes. Serve at once or refrigerate.

Banana-Lemon Sundae Sauce

Preparation time: 4 minutes

Cooking time: 6 minutes

Servings: 2 cups

Ingredients:

2 large firm bananas, sliced (about 2 cups sliced)

1 tsp lemon juice

½ cup butter

1½ cups confectioners' sugar

1 tbsp water

1 tsp vanilla extract

¼ tsp ground cinnamon

Vanilla ice cream

Directions:

1. Melt the butter in a small saucepan then whisk in the lemon juice, confectioners' sugar and water until very smooth.

2. Cook for 3 to 5 minutes over medium-low heat, stirring offten then remove from the heat. Stir in the cinnamon and vanilla then whisk the banana slices.

3. Serve warm on top of the ice cream.

Chocó Walnut-Cinnamon Sundaes

Preparation time: 5 minutes

Cooking time: 15 minutes + chilling time

Servings: 4 (1 cup)

Ingredients:

½ cup chocolate chips, semi-sweet

1 tsp ground cinnamon

1 cup diced walnuts

½ cup butter

1/3 cup brown sugar, packed

¼ cup half and half cream

¼ cup corn syrup

1 tsp vanilla extract

Vanilla ice cream

Directions:

1. Mix all the ingredients together except vanilla, cinnamon and walnut in a small saucepan then bring to a boil over medium-low heat, stirring consistently. Lower the heat then cook for another 5 minutes, stirring often. Remove the mixture from heat then stir in the vanilla and cinnamon.

2. Pour the mixture into a heat-proof measuring cup then cool for 10 minutes, stirring once in a while. Pour your sauce over the vanilla ice cream then garnish with the chopped walnuts.

3. Store leftover sauce in the refrigerator then warm in the microwave before using.

Creamy Vanilla Apple Sundae

Preparation time: 5 minutes

Cooking time: 15 minutes

Servings: 4 to 6

Ingredients:

5 cups of peeled tart apple thin slices

1 cup brown sugar, packed

3 tbsp butter

1 tsp vanilla extract

¼ cup all-purpose flour

¼ cup water

1 tbsp lemon juice

½ tsp salt

Vanilla ice cream

Directions:

1. Mix flour, brown sugar, lemon juice, water and salt in a large saucepan then stir until smooth. Bring the mixture to a boil then stir for 2 minutes or until it becomes thick. Add the sliced apples then continue boiling. Lower the heat, cover then simmer for 10 to 12 minutes or until the apples become soft.

2. Remove the sauce from heat then add the butter and vanilla. Stir the sauce until the butter completely dissolves.

3. Serve topping warm or at room temperature over the ice cream.

Cinnamon-Pear Topping

Preparation time: 5 minutes

Cooking time: 15 minutes

Servings: 6

Ingredients:

29 oz. pear halves

2/3 cup brown sugar, packed

1 tsp ground cinnamon

¼ cup butter, cubed

Vanilla ice cream

Directions:

1. Mix butter, brown sugar and cinnamon together in a saucepan then cook for 5 minutes over medium heat, stirring until the butter dissolves.

2. Drain the pears and reserve ½ cup of the juice, throw away the remaining juice or store for another use.

3. Pour the reserved juice and pears into a saucepan then cook for 8 to 10 minutes or until well heated.

4. Serve the topping warm over ice cream.

Vanilla Peanut Ice Cream Topping

Preparation time: 5 minutes

Cooking time: 15 minutes

Servings: 20 (makes 3½ cups)

Ingredients:

1 cup peanuts, dry-roasted (or preferred nuts like pecans, plain peanuts or cashews)

4 tsp cornstarch

¼ cup butter or margarine

1½ cups evaporated milk

½ cup corn syrup, light-colored

1 cup brown sugar, packed

1 tsp vanilla

Directions:

1. Mix milk and cornstarch together in a medium saucepan then add the butter/margarine and corn syrup. Cook over medium heat, stirring until it becomes thick and bubbly then cook for another 2 minutes, stirring.

2. Remove the sauce from heat then stir in the vanilla and brown sugar. Let it slightly cool for about 5 to 10 minutes.

3. Stir in the nuts then serve warm over the ice cream.

4. You may allow the sauce cool in a container, cover then refrigerate for up to a week. When ready to serve, Microwave 1 cup of the sauce on high temperature for 1 to 1½ minutes or reheat in a saucepan over low heat until warm, stir once.

Creamy Marshmallow Topping

Preparation time: 5 minutes

Cooking time: 15 minutes

Servings: 4 to 6

Ingredients:

8 oz. marshmallows

2 tbsp water

¾ cup sugar

¼ cup milk

1 tbsp light corn syrup

1 tsp vanilla extract

Directions:

1. Dissolve the marshmallows in water on top of a double boiler over hot water not boiling water then leave in on top then set it aside.

2. Mix milk, sugar and corn syrup together in a heavy saucepan then bring to a boil. Lower the heat then simmer for 5 minutes. Pour the mixture over the marshmallows.

3. Pour the marshmallow back into the mixture then heat on low heat then mix whisk, hand mixer or egg beater until it becomes smooth. The sauce will become thick as it cooks.

4. Remove the sauce from heat then stir in the vanilla extract. Serve over ice cream at room temperature.

Chocó Espresso Sauce

Preparation time: 5 minutes

Cooking time: 15 minutes

Servings: 3½ cups

Ingredients:

8 oz. white chocolate, chopped in pieces

2 cups heavy cream

3½ tbsp instant espresso powder

Directions:

1. Combine all the ingredients in a small heavy-bottom saucepan then heat over medium heat until the chocolate starts to dissolve then lower the heat to low.

2. Stir the chocolate until it completely dissolves then remove the sauce from heat. Whisk the sauce actively until it becomes thick and very smooth. Set the sauce aside to cool to room temperature.

3. Pour the sauce into a small pitcher, cover then refrigerate until chilled. Stir then pour over the ice cream.

Sweet Peanut Butter Sundae

Preparation time: 5 minutes

Cooking time: 10 minutes

Servings: 4

Ingredients:

2/3 cup peanut butter

1/3 cup white sugar

1/3 cup water

Directions:

1. In a small saucepan, combine the white sugar and water then heat over high heat then bring to a boil. Boil the mixture for 1 minute then remove from heat then stir in the peanut butter until it completely dissolves until well mixed.

2. Pour the warm sauce over the ice cream then serve.

Creamy Banana-Strawberry Ice Cream Sauce

Strawberry and banana is the right combination for that fruity and delicious ice cream topping.

Preparation time: 5 minutes

Cooking time: 25 minutes

Servings: 2

Ingredients:

1 lb strawberries, remove the stems then chop

1 banana, diced

1 tablespoon lemon juice

1/3 heaping cup sugar

2 teaspoons cornstarch

1/3 cup water + 3 tablespoons

Directions:

1. Mix the strawberries, lemon juice, banana, 1/3 cup plus 2 tbsp of water and the sugar together in a pan then bring to a boil. Lower the heat then simmer for about 20 minutes.

2. Now, mix the cornstarch and 1 tbsp of water together into a syrup then pour the mixture into the strawberry mixture then simmer for some minutes or until thick enough to coat the back of a spoon.

3. Scoop the mixture into 2 8-oz. jars then chill in the refrigerator until cold.

4. Serve the sauce over your ice cream.

Brandy Blackberry Sundae

Preparation time: 5 minutes

Cooking time: 20 minutes

Servings: 4

Ingredients:

1 tbsp brandy

4 cups fresh blackberries

2 tbsp cornstarch

1 cup sugar

¼ cup of water

Directions:

1. In a saucepan, mix the blackberries, brandy and sugar together then set over medium heat then bring to a simmer slowly. Cook for about 10 minutes until the blackberries become tender.

2. Melt the cornstarch in water then stir the mixture into the simmering berries. Continue cooking for about 10 minutes, stirring until the sauce becomes thick and gets to your desired texture.

Vanilla Grape Ice Cream Sauce

Preparation time: 10 minutes

Cooking time: 10 minutes

Servings: 6

Ingredients:

2 cups concord grapes

½ tsp vanilla extract

½ cup of water

½ tsp butter

¼ cup granulated sugar

½ tbsp cornstarch

1 tbsp water

1 pinch of salt

Directions:

1. Pour the whole grapes into a medium-size saucepan then pour in ½ cup of water to cover the base of the pan.

2. Bring the grapes to a boil then cook for about 5 minutes. Remove the mixture from heat then strain through a cheese cloth, reserve about 1 cup of the juice then throw away the seeds and skins.

3. In a small dish, combine cornstarch and 1 tbsp of water then set aside.

4. Pour the reserved juice back into the saucepan then heat over low heat. Add the cornstarch mixture and sugar then bring to a boil until the juice becomes thick.

5. Remove the juice from heat then add the butter, pinch of salt and vanilla.

6. Serve the topping warm over the ice cream.

7. You may refrigerate the topping then warm in a microwave before using.

Cooking tip: Refrigerating the sauce makes it thick like a jelly texture then microwave for about 30 to 60 seconds before using.

Creamy Vanilla Nutella Ice Cream Topping

Preparation time: 5 minutes

Cooking time: 15 minutes

Servings: 1 cup

Ingredients:

½ cup heavy cream

2 tbsp butter

3 tbsp Nutella

1 tsp vanilla

½ cup sugar

¼ tsp salt

Directions:

1. Mix the cream, sugar, nutella and salt together in a medium-size pot then heat over medium heat.

2. Cook, stirring until the nutella melts into the cream

3. Add the butter to the hot cream mixture then stir until well mixed.

4. Bring the sauce to a boil, stirring consistently then bring to a boil for 2 minutes.

5. Remove the sauce from heat then stir in the vanilla

6. Now, the sauce will be bubbly and extremely hot. Let it cool until a bit warm before pouring over your ice cream.

Creamy Nutty Ice Cream Sauce

Preparation time: 5 minutes

Cooking time: 10 minutes

Servings: 16

Ingredients:

2 cups chopped walnuts, or whole (or 2 cups chopped pecans, or whole)

1 cup white corn syrup

1 tsp vanilla

1 cup brown sugar

3 tbsp butter

½ cup milk

Directions:

1. Bring the corn syrup, butter, brown sugar and milk to a gentle boil over medium heat, stirring properly.

2. Boil the mixture lightly for 5 minutes then remove the sauce from heat.

3. Stir in the nuts and vanilla properly then let it cool.

Concluded

Printed in Great Britain
by Amazon